HOME PRESERVING RECIPES

*A Foolproof Guide to Conservation, Preserved Meats,
Fruits And Sugar Free Jams*

by Susan Lombardi

Copyright 2022 by Susan Lombardi

All rights reserved

The content of this book may not be reproduce, duplicated or transmitted without direct written permission from the author or the publisher.

Under no circumstances will any blame or legal responsibility be held against the publisher or author, for any damages, reparation or monetary loss due the information contains within this book.

Legal Notice:

This book is copyright protected and is only for personal use. You cannot amend, distribute, sell, use or quote any part of this book without the consent of the author or the publisher.

Disclaimer Notice:

Please note the information contained within this document is for educational purpose only. All effort has been executed to present accurate, up to date and reliable, complete information. No warranties of any kind are declared or implied. Readers acknowledge that the author is not engaging in the rendering of legal, financial, medical or professional advice. The content within this book has been derived from various sources. Please consult a licensed professional before attempting any techniques outlined in this book. By reading this document, the reader agrees that under no circumstances is the author responsible for any losses, direct or indirect, which are incurred as a result of the use of information contained within this document, including, but not limited to, errors, omissions or inaccuracies.

TABLE OF CONTENTS

INTRODUCTION

There is no other time to learn how to preserve food safely at home than now. Whether growing your food or buying in bulk, you can stock up on food and save money by home food preservation.It can add variety to your meals and make them taste better than most supermarket products. You have control over what goes into your food. This book will help you decide which home food preservation method is best for you.

Excellent storage is one example of an old home food preservation method. Others, such as freeze-drying, are more recent. Safety concerns have led to some home food preservation methods being dropped.

This book contains a variety of food preservation options. Each method has a unique flavor and texture. Different foods can also be stored in different ways.Ingredients play a significant role in the safety and quality of home-preserved food. The first step is to select the best quality fruits and vegetables at their freshest. Avoid those that are brittle or have signs of decay. Follow preservation instructions precisely as they are written. It would help if you did not alter the amounts or ratios of ingredients that can affect acidity or texture, as these factors are critical to the safety and effectiveness of the preservation process. Only minor changes are allowed if the recipe permits. This guide contains information about many common ingredients used in home food preservation recipes. It doesn't have to be difficult to preserve food, but it is essential to practice good food safety to prevent foodborne illness.

CHAPTER ONE: WHAT IS FOOD PRESERVATION?

Food preservation is "the science that deals with preventing spoilage or decay of food and allowing it to be stored in a suitable condition for future use." Preservation preserves the nutritional value, quality, and edibility of food. Preservation prevents bacteria, fungi, and other microorganisms from growing. It also includes retarding oxidation to reduce rancidity. This process ensures that there are no discoloration and no aging. Sealing is also necessary to stop microbes from returning. Food preservation ensures food stays:

- In the same state as when purchased.
- Not contaminated with pathogenic organisms and chemicals
- Do not lose its best qualities of color, texture, and flavor.

Food Preserving Benefits

Everyone is trying to find ways to cut down on food costs, especially with the increasing cost of food. Home food preserving is one of my favorite things. Food preservation can be expensive at first. These items can last a lifetime. Our civilization has prioritized finding ways to preserve food during times of excess for consumption in the lean months. The benefits of our ancestors' efforts to keep food are still a positive influence on our lives today. We're also gaining new benefits. The modern benefits of food preservation have a broad impact on our lives, communities, and the environment. Here are some reasons to preserve your home's food.

- Food preservation is the prevention of food spoilage by enzymes and microorganisms.
- Food preservation extends the shelf life of food.
- This increases the availability of out-of-season foodstuffs.
- It makes it possible to access various food products even if they are not readily available. It makes it easier to transport food materials.

- Food preservation compensates for any deficiencies in the diet.

Therefore, we can conclude that food preservation techniques are the best way to preserve different foods. Food preservation aims to prevent microbial growth, extend shelf life and maintain food safety.

CHAPTER TWO: TIPS FOR FOOD SAFETY

People all over the globe are practicing social isolation and self-distancing at home. This means more home-cooked food and a greater need to learn proper food storage, handling, and cooking techniques.It's becoming more common to cook at home. This means that it is essential to maintain the highest standards. The latest science confirms that the coronavirus cannot be transmitted through food. However, food safety tips avoid foodborne illnesses like E—Coli, Salmonella, and yeast.

1. Avoid Overpacking Your Fridge

Although it may seem tempting to stuff your fridge with many stockpiled groceries, air circulation is essential to keep food cool. You can use a thermometer to ensure that food is kept at 40°F (4°C). This could mean that the fridge temperature should be adjusted to 40° F (4° C). You should not overpack your fridge. However, a freezer will work more efficiently if it is complete.

2. Make Sure You Load Your Fridge Strategically

You can designate a drawer for raw meat that you want to freeze in the refrigerator. This will prevent juices from traveling to other places than the drawer or container. Pre-cooked or plant-based meats should not be stored next to avoid cross-contamination. Before putting fresh produce away, wash and rinse it. Pro tip: Before storing plastic containers and bottles in your fridge or pantry, wipe them clean with a sanitizing cloth.

3. Let Leftovers Cool Down Before Storing

There is an easy way to store leftovers safely. Proper storage requires that fragments are not left at room temperature for more than two hours. The remaining food should be stored in smaller, 1-inch-2-inch deep containers. After cooling, place the container in the refrigerator.

4. Keep Track Of When Your Leftovers In The Freezer Or Fridge Will Expire

The remaining pieces in the refrigerator should be consumed within three to four days. You can freeze leftovers if you don't intend to eat them immediately. You can put pieces in the freezer for up to three months. *Pro tip: Label all containers with the storage date to make it easy to identify when you need to throw them out.*

5. How To Properly Freeze Frozen Food

These are various ways to freeze and thaw food properly.

- Thaw in the fridge. Keep the juices from raw meat out of your fridge. This method requires that most foods are thawed within four to five hours.
- Put the food in cold water and then run under it. To prevent the food from becoming too warm, change the water every 30 mins if you are freezing food. This process can take up to 30 minutes per pound. This method should only be used if the food is cooked immediately afterward.

- You can either freeze or defrost the food in the microwave. This method should only be used if the food is cooked immediately afterward. Follow the instructions on your microwave or use defrost.

- When thawing frozen food, ensure that the temperature inside the food does not reach the "danger zone." This is between 40° F (4°C) and 140°F (60°C). This can cause bacteria to multiply and lead to foodborne illness.

- Never thaw food at room temperature or on the countertop. This can lead to uneven temperatures.

- Cooking from frozen meats and poultry will result in approximately half the cooking time.

6. Pay Attention To Expiration Dates

There is so much more preserved food around the house. Look closely at expiration dates to understand the differences between best by, use before, and expired by dates. Food safety: Expiration and use-by dates. These dates should not be exceeded.

- **Sell-by dates**: These are guidelines for retailers that allow them to know the maximum time an item can be displayed for sale.

- **Use by dates**: These are guidelines for how long a product can retain its peak quality and freshness.

7. Clean High-Touch Surfaces With The Entire Family

Are you having trouble keeping your children occupied at school? Children make great helpers when it comes to sanitizing the house. You can challenge them to identify all common touch points in the home, such as countertops, refrigerator handles and knobs on the kitchen cabinets, faucet handles, light switches, panel buttons, and panel buttons. Adults can disinfect and clean the touch points.

8. Wash Your Hands

Proper handwashing is the best way to prevent germs from spreading. As the global number of COVID-19 patients continues to rise, it is important to keep your eyes on what you can control. Food safety, hygiene, and cleanliness in your home are all areas you can control and will help you ensure your safety and health.

9. Food Preservation Time

To avoid food waste and maximize nutrition, it is vital to understand the shelf life of frozen and home-preserved food. Keep your preserved food fresh and delicious. When you have excess fresh produce, preserving food is a good idea. Make sure that you can use your frozen or preserved food within the time limit. Properly preserved foods can last for many years, but their nutritional and quality value will decrease with time. According to the National Center for Home Food Preservation, food should be preserved for at least one year. Your home-preserved food should taste great and be nutritious when you eat it.

CHAPTER THREE:
FOOD PRESERVING - TOOLS AND EQUIPMENT

Understanding the classifications will make finding the right tools for preservation easier. It can take time to collect all the equipment and tools needed for food preservation. The supplies required for food preservation can be found in most grocery stores, department stores, or restaurant supply shops (though some restaurant supply stores may require wholesale orders). Sometimes, larger appliances such as deep freezes can also be used to preserve food.

Canning utensils are much more efficient than traditional kitchen utensils for preserving food. It is good to keep your set in a container with a lid to ensure they are safe and easy to access when you need them.

Hot Water Bath Canner: A hot water bath canner will be used to process high-acidic foods such as tomatoes, pickles, or fruits.

Pressure Canner: A pressure canner is required for low-acid foods such as meat, vegetables, or dairy. Pressure canners must be used to preserve seafood, meats, poultry, and vegetables safely.

Blanching & Steaming Basket: This steamer basket is perfect for canned, frozen, or dried blanched foods. This versatile accessory can fit in any pressure cooker or instant pot.

Glass Jars & Lids: You can keep your food safe and beautiful displayed by using high-quality lids and jars. You should stay various sizes available depending on the type of food you are preserving. Pots can be reused, but covers will need replacing.

Mylar Bags & Oxygen Absorbers: Mylar bags are available in various sizes and can be used for dry goods storage in individual containers or 5-gallon buckets. Mylar bags and jars are kept airy with oxygen absorbers. They are used with all my freeze-dried foods. The size of your suitcase or jar will determine how big oxygen absorbers you need.

Mylar Bag Sealer: Mylar bags can also be sealed with heat using an iron, flat iron, or impulse sealer. Some mylar bags can be filled with a vacuum sealer, but most mylar bags will require a higher heat setting.

Food Processor Or Blender: High-quality food processors and blenders will reduce the time it takes to prepare foods for preservation.

Home Freeze-Dryer: This is my favorite and the most expensive recommendation I have. Because it is an essential part of my food preservation plan, my Harvest Right freeze-dryer works almost 24 hours per day.

CHAPTER FOUR: TYPES OF FOOD PRESERVATION

There are many types of food preservation:

1. Fermentation

Fermentation transforms low-acid foods into high-acid foods. They can also be stored "as is" for longer shelf life or can be canned in a water bath canner instead of a pressure canner. Salt, whey, and specific starter cultures can help food ferment. This makes food easier to digest and provides more nutrients. Fermented food is also called "live culture food." Fermentation involves the use of acidity and microbes to "pre-digest" food. This results in a change in the flavor and texture. Fermentation is used to create yogurt, chocolate, yogurt, and Kombucha. It also helps produce pantry staples such as sauerkraut and kimchi.

2. Freezing

Freezing refers to the preservation of prepared food items in cold storage. Freezing is one way to start food preservation. You don't have to worry about sealing jars or ensuring that your ingredients are in the proper ratio. You don't need to have a lot of space. Frozen herbs can take up as much space as a tray full of ice cubes. You can freeze frozen corn flat in freezer bags. This makes it easier to slide into small spaces. You don't need special equipment to freeze foods, so it is easy for beginners. Most vegetables need to be blanched or cooked before freezing. This prevents enzyme action and preserves quality. The freezing method uses freezing temperature for various food items to protect them. This can extend their life expectancy up to several weeks or even a month. The same as chilling, freezing uses specific measures to extend the shelf life of food items, such as food storage and freezing temperature. Food that has been stored in an airtight container, frozen at -18 to 20 degrees Celsius, and regularly defrosted can extend its shelf life by at least one month

You should follow these steps to freeze food safely:

- Adjust the freezer temperature to between -18 and -22 degrees Celsius
- Before freezing food, place it in freezer bags or airtight containers. Wrapping meat properly is crucial, as it can get frozen, burnt, and unusable.
- Do not freeze any items after their best before date or use-by date.
- Defrosted food should not be refrigerated as bacteria can grow in between thawing. It is best to either use it immediately or keep it in the refrigerator for 24 hours.
- To prevent ice buildup, defrost your freezer frequently. Frozen food should be kept in the refrigerator for two hours while it defrosts.
- Label food with the date it was frozen. Refer to the date to determine if the food should be used before it deteriorates.

3. Blanching

Blanching is the heat treatment of vegetables followed by immersion in cold water to stop them from cooking. Expected blanching times are three minutes in boiling water. To prolong storage life and prevent discoloration, fruits can be frozen "as-is." Both vegetable and fruit preservation are my favorite. I freeze food on a cookie sheet, then seal them in vacuum-sealed packages for long-term storage. Vacuum sealing frozen produce can prevent ice crystal formation and extends the shelf life by up to five times. It is a good idea to vacuum seal all frozen foods.

4. Freeze-Drying

How does a home freezer dryer work?

- You first get a Heavy Duty freezer (the Harvest Right units are -30°F (-34°C) or colder).
- You pair it with an airtight chamber that can keep a vacuum (no oxygen) every time you use it.
- The third step is to attach a high-end vacuum pump powerful enough to suck the stripes from a zebra.
- Fourth, you install a thermostat and heater so that you can adjust the temperature and repeat the sublimation process over and over again for hours.
- Fifth, attach a humidity sensor to prevent water from the system and trigger the cycle.

You can freeze-dry many foods at home, including dairy products, whole meals, soups made with cream, and leftovers. You can also store fruits, vegetables, meats, and seafood.

5. Drying/Dehydrating

Drying this is also known as dehydration. It is one of the oldest methods for food preservation. This method decreases water activity, which stops bacterial growth. Drying helps reduce weight, making it easier to transport food. Both sun and wind can be used to dry. This method can dry meat and fruits like grapes, apricots, and apples. It removes moisture from food through natural sunlight. The ancients used drying methods to dry spices, fruits, and vegetables. The sun's powerful light can be used to dry the items.You must have heard of the sundried tomato, which originated in Southern Italy and is famous for its sweet flavor.

You can dry food using:

- Commercial dehydrators such as the Excalibur and American Harvest Dehydrator are available.
- Solar dehydrators
- Sun Ovens
- Baking sheets in the oven
- Air drying/hang drying

Dry foods work well when space is limited, but not all foods can dehydrate well. Dehydrated foods should be kept in a dry, cool place in an airtight container to ensure the most extended shelf life.

These foods can be dehydrated well:

- Fruits
- Vegetables
- Fruit Leathers
- Jerky

6. Curing And Smoking

This is a traditional food preservation method that uses smoke from burning a particular type of wood to preserve food. Smoked food items are flavored with the unique flavors of formaldehyde and phenolic compounds from the wood. Smoking is used mainly for meats and fish. The antimicrobial properties and phenolic compounds preserve the food.

7. Salt And Sugar

Before modern freezing, canning, and dehydrating became available, salt and sugar were used to preserve foods. Salt and sugar strip liquid from food. This can hinder microbe growth. Salt and sugar preservation are great for adventurous palates, as they can dramatically alter the flavor and texture of foods. You can easily preserve fresh herbs by making herb-infused sugars and salts. Most sugaring is used to preserve fruits such as cranberries, mangoes, and apricots and is commonly known as jam. Sugar is added to fruits to increase sugar concentration. This causes the food item's water content to drop and protects it from microbial attack.

All sugary substances can be used, including sugar syrup, sugar granules, and honey. Besides fruits, vegetables such as ginger and carrots can also be preserved with sugaring. These can then be used to make condiments.To preserve certain foods, some sugaring recipes use alcohol in addition to sugar.

8. Salting

It is similar to sugaring—salting results in the release of water from the food, preventing harmful microorganisms' growth. There are two types of salting: dry curing and wet curing. Dry curing is when salt is added to food items such as fish, meat, and chicken. It is used to extract water from it.

A salt solution or brine is used to preserve vegetables for extended periods. This is in contrast to wet curing. Salting and sugaring are two food preservation techniques requiring special attention because excessive salt or sugar can pose health risks.

9. Immersion In Alcohol

Alcohol, like salt and sugar, draws water from food. This inhibits microbe growth. Small amounts of food can be submerged in the hard liquor you choose, and they will keep almost indefinitely. Do not try to preserve too many foods in too little alcohol. There is a limit on how much water you can absorb. This method of food preservation is ideal for creating flavor extracts and preserving high-acid foods like fruit.

10. Immersion in oil

Although this home food preservation technique is quite common in some parts of Europe, it is not recommended for home preservers who aren't experienced. To preserve food, oil is used to cover it.

CHAPTER FIVE: HINTS ABOUT CANNING

Canning is a step beyond cooking. This is the process of heating food in closed canners for home canning to prevent any natural spoilage and remove any air to seal the jar. This is also known as bottling. Many types of canners sterilize the pots and the food materials inside. Water bath canners can be used to preserve high-acid foods, while pressure canners can keep low-acid foods. Different food items can be canned, such as vegetables, fruits, and meat. First, they are processed and then placed in a sterilized can or jar. The top lid seals the jars and can be labeled with information such as the date of processing or the name of each food item.

You can start canning with what you're most likely to eat. It's easy to make instant pot applesauce, which is more interesting than what you buy in a grocery store. If you're a bit too enthusiastic about your garden planting, our method of storing winter squash is the best. Making pumpkin puree at home will add more flavor to your favorite fall baking recipes.

What Supplies Are Needed For My Canning Recipes

- Jars, lids, and rings. You need to be able to can. Canning jars can be found in almost all grocery and hardware stores.
- Large stock pot or water bath canner. You will need to immerse the jars in boiling water to make them shelf-stable. You can use any large bank. Many "canners" that you can find are just large stock pots with a rack inside. You don't need the stand if you have a large pot. It protects your jars and ensures that your food is cooked through.).
- Jar lifter. Wet glass jars can be slippery. Get a good jar lifting tool for a few dollars.
- You will need dish towels, knives, cutting boards, colanders, and other kitchen tools. You probably have everything you need to can in your kitchen.

What Are The Benefits Of Home Food Canning?

- **Save Money**: Food can be costly. You can save money by buying fresh produce and canning them for later use. This is especially true if you consider the quality of your food.

- **Know what you're eating:** You can put whatever you like in your home food canner. Home-canned fruits and vegetables can be preserved without colorings, preservatives, or other additives.

- Everything goes into your food. You can choose organic produce and control the sugar used. This also allows you to improve the flavor and texture of your food.

- **Foods with better taste:** Homemade food tastes better, and it's a known fact. A quality canned product from home made with fresh ingredients is unbeatable. You could pay twice as much in the grocery store for the same product. Home food canning has another advantage: you can customize recipes to suit your tastes and experiment with new flavors.

Types of Home Canning

There are three types of home canning:

1. Water Bath Canning: A large stockpot or kettle is required for water bath canning. The jars are placed in a canning rack or other material not to touch the pot's bottom. Canning high-alcohol foods with a water bath (pH 4.6 or lower) are possible by canning.

- Fruits
- Jams, jelly, and other spreads
- Tomatoes with added acid
- Pickles and relishes

2. Steam Canning: Steam canning has been reapproved for home use. It uses a particular canner that heats with steam but not under pressure. It can be used with high-acid foods.

3. Pressure Canning: A pressure canner is required for pressure canning. High-pressure steam is used for canned foods at high temperatures. Although a pressure canner isn't the same as a pressure cooker, some canners can be used for pressure cooking. Some cooperative extension offices offer pressure cooker testing. Pressure canning is not perfect for low-acid foods like.

- Beans
- Carrots
- Corn
- Meats
- Soups
- Sauces
- Broth

Unsafe canning practices can cause botulism poisoning, but this can easily be avoided using trusted canning recipes.

Food Canning Process

Canning food can significantly increase life expectancy, but only if correctly done. Canning preserves food by sealing it tightly and keeping it in an acidic, sugary, or salty environment that prevents bacteria from growing. It is essential to follow safe and proper canning procedures such as:

- Choose good quality food that has not been used or is in its best before date. It should be handled with care.

- Only purchase canning jars with self-sealing lids suitable for your purpose. Old jam pots and peanut butter jars cannot be reused as they don't guarantee an airtight seal.
- Purchase a canning rack.
- Use tested preservation methods.

Steps To Canning

To ensure the safe preservation of canned foods, you must carefully follow each step outlined in this book.

- Warm the jars in boiling water before heating.
- Follow the preservation recipe to prepare the food. Food should be heated to boiling.
- Take the jars out of the water and fill them with the food.
- You may fill the jar with food, depending on the recipe. You may have to put jam in the jar or add acidic liquids or brines that you will boil before you fill it.
- Allow 1/2 inch headspace before applying the sealing lid. The lid should be adjusted until it fits snugly around the fingertip.
- Pour boiling water into the jars using the canning rack. This will take place for the time specified in the recipe.
- Take out the pieces and let them cool.
- You can adjust the processing time based on the altitude chart.

Boiling Water Bath Canner: Altitude Adjustments

1 - 3,000 feet	3,001 to 6,001 feet	6,001 to 8,000 feet	8.001 to 10,000 feet
5 minutes	10 minutes	15 minutes	20 minutes

CHAPTER SIX:
SIMPLE RECIPES FOR QUICK MEALS

MEAT

Preserving Simple Meatballs

Preparation Time: 1 hour

Cooking Time: 40 minutes

Ingredients for 40 meatballs:

- 300 g high-quality pork sausage
- 1 small onion
- 1 carrot
- 1 tbsp dried oregano
- 500 g minced lean beef
- 50 g Parmesan, finely grated, plus an extra to serve

- 75 g dry breadcrumb
- 1 medium egg
- 1 tbsp olive oil

To make tomato sauce:

- 1 finely grated carrot
- 2 sticks of celery (grated)
- 1 courgette (coarsely grated)
- 3 cloves of garlic (finely grated)
- 2 red peppers
- 1 tbsp olive oil
- 1 tbsp tomato puree
- pinch golden caster sugar
- Red wine vinegar is a great choice
- 3 x 400 g tins chopped tomato
- A snipped handful of basil leaves
- Spaghetti cooked to order

Instructions:

1. Take all the sausagemeat from the skins and place it in a large bowl. You can either hold the links or squash them on a board.
2. Grate the onion and finely grated carrot. These vegetables should be tossed in with the sausages. Set aside the Parmesan, garlic, and other vegetables you have grated while the grater is still used.
3. Mix everything to make an excellent mixture. Next, combine all meatball ingredients except olive oil in a bowl. Season with black pepper

4. Mix everything with your hands until it is all combined.

5. Roll the meatball mixture into small walnut-sized balls and place them on a tray or board. You can cover the meatballs with cling wrap and give them a good clean-up.

6. Make sure to prepare the red peppers. First, remove the skins from the peppers using a vegetable peeler. Next, remove the seeds and cut the tops and bottoms. The peppers can be cut into strips.

7. Make the sauce. In a large saucepan, heat the oil. Cook the vegetables and garlic for 5 minutes. Mix in the tomato puree and sugar. Let it sit for 1 minute, then add the tomatoes. Allow simmering for 5 minutes. Next, use a hand blender to blend the sauce. While you prepare the meatballs, simmer the sauce gently.

8. The meatballs should be cooked. The meatballs can be browned in olive oil. Once they are browned, add them to the sauce. Let the meatballs simmer in the sauce for 15 minutes, occasionally stirring until they are done. You can either eat it right away or let it cool in a container and freeze for up to 6 months. If you prefer, serve with spaghetti, basil, and extra Parmesan.

Nutritional Values Per Serving

Kcal	Fat	Satured	Carbs	Sugars
375	21 g	8 g	21 g	11 g

Fibers	Proteins	Salt
4 g	25 g	1.5 g

Preserving Beef Hotpot

Preparation Time: 5 minutes

Cooking Time: 45 minutes

Ingredients For 5 Servings:

- 2 onions
- 300 g carrots
- 1 kg potatoes
- 450 g minced lean beef
- 2 beef stock cubes
- Baked beans: 400 g
- A splash of Worcestershire sauce
- *A handful of chopped parsley, optional*

Instructions:

1. Each onion should be cut into eight wedges. Cut the carrots into small pieces. Chop the potatoes in large chunks. Turn on the kettle.

2. In a large nonstick skillet, heat the mince. Once the mince is browned, quickly stir the mixture. Mix well. Add the stock cubes. Mix the vegetables, and then add 900ml/1 1/2 liters of boiling water to the kettle. Bring to boil

3. Cover the pan and let the vegetables simmer on low heat for about 25-30 minutes. Add the baked beans and a good splash of Worcestershire sauce, and heat through. If necessary, taste and adjust the salt and pepper.

4. Sprinkle the parsley over the hotpot, and then serve it in bowls. You can place the Worcestershire sauce bottle on your table for those who want a little more spice.

5. You can either eat it right away or let it cool in a container and freeze for four months.

Nutritional Values Per Serving

Kcal	Fat	Satured	Carbs
417	10 g	4 g	55 g

Sugars	Fibers	Proteins	Salt
3 g	8 g	29 g	2.9 g

Preserving Jerky

Preparation Time: 60 minutes

Cooking Time: 3 hours

Ingredients:

- 1 kg+ of meat
- 4 crushed garlic cloves
- 1 cup wine, beer, or soy sauce
- 2 tsp sea salt (omit if you are using soy sauce)
- 1 cup cider vinegar or lemon juice
- 1/4 c Worcestershire sauce
- 1/4 cup brown sugar
- 1/4 tsp
- 1 tsp dry mustard
- 1 tbsp liquid smoke

- 2 tsp Spices (oregano and mint, basil, thyme. thyme. sage. Tumeric. cumin. chives. parsley. etc.)
- *1/2 tsp Ground chili (optional)*

Instructions:

1. Remove the bones from the meat
2. Reduce excess fat
3. Cut 1/4-inch strips from your meat
4. Place in a casserole dish or deep bowl
5. Make your marinade
6. Use different spices in different batches to create variety
7. Pour marinade over meat in a deep bowl or casserole
8. Cover and refrigerate overnight or for at least 4 hours
9. Place on dehydrator tray
10. Dry at 155°F for 6-8 hours and then turn after 3 hours
11. To ensure even drying, move the dehydrator trays around as needed
12. Continue drying the meat until it is crisp and dry, without any moist spots
13. Keep it in a sealed container in a dry, cool place for up to a year

Nutritional Values Per Serving

Kcal	Fat	Carbs	Sugars	Fibers	Proteins	Salt
524	51 g	34 g	0 g	2 g	31 g	1.38 g

Preserving Balsamic Beef Stew

Preparation Time: 30 minutes

Cooking Time: 2 hours

Ingredients For 8-10 Servings:

- 2 1/2 pounds stew beef, excellent quality
- Good quality Balsamic Vinegar: 1 to 2 cups
- 2 tablespoons olive oils
- 2 bay leaves
- 1 teaspoon fresh thyme, 1 1/2 teaspoons dried
- 2 cloves of garlic, chopped fine
- 1 can of tomato paste
- 1 1/2 teaspoons chopped fresh rosemary leaves
- 2 cups Beef Stock, homemade preferred
- 3 cups red wine (such as Burgundy, Barolo, or other varieties)

- 1/2 cup water
- 1 lb small red potatoes skin-unpeeled and cut into bite-size pieces
- 1 lb carrots cut into 1-inch slices
- 2 small onions, quartered
- 1 pound of small mushrooms, quartered
- 1 cup chopped fresh parsley
- Add some coarse salt to the dish and some freshly ground black pepper to taste
- *3 tablespoons water, 3 tablespoons cornstarch (optional)*

Instructions:

1. Add the stew meat cubes and balsamic vinegar and toss in a large bowl. Allow marinating for at least one night in the refrigerator. Once ready to use the balsamic vinegar, drain it off and discard.

2. Olive oil can be added to a large, heavy saucepan over medium heat. Brown the stew meat on all sides. Drain any liquid accumulated during browning and place it in a bowl. You can then add it back later.

3. Reduce heat to medium-low. Cook the garlic, bay leaves, thyme, and tomato paste until fragrant.

4. Add the beef stock, wine, rosemary leaves, and water. Cover the pot with a lid. Bring to a boil on medium heat. Reduce heat to medium. Let it simmer for about 1 1/2 hours, or until the meat is tender but not falling apart. You can check on the heart now and again to ensure that liquid doesn't evaporate. If necessary, add a little more water. The juice should be concentrated with flavor.

5. Stews should be cooked at low temperatures. The liquid's surface should not move. The fat from rich meats will melt if you simmer the dish gently. You can then chill the word and skim off any excess fat.

6. Add the potatoes, carrots, and onions once the stew beef has been cooked. Return to a simmer. Cook for approximately 45 minutes, stirring occasionally or until all vegetables are tender. *Optional: If you desire a thicker stew, you can add the cornstarch mixture at this stage.* Mix the mixture until it becomes slightly thickened.

7. Salt and pepper to your liking.

8. To soak up the juice, serve with some good sourdough bread and a simple green salad or freeze in the freezer for 2 months.

Nutritional Values Per Serving

Kcal	Fat	Carbs	Sugars	Fibers	Proteins	Salt
619	47 g	34 g	0 g	2 g	39 g	1.38 g

Preserving Beef and Barley Stew

Preparation Time: 30 minutes

Cooking Time: 2 hours

Ingredients For 10 Servings:

- 3 pounds of stew beef cut into bite-sized pieces
- 1/2 cup red wine vinegar
- 2 cups of water
- 2 teaspoons coarse sea salt
- 3 cloves garlic, minced
- 1 large Spanish onion, peeled & diced
- 2 ribs celery, diced
- 6 carrots, peeled & sliced
- 1/2 pound pearl barley
- 1 cup Shiraz wine
- 1 (8-ounce) can of tomato paste
- 8 cups Beef Stock
- 2 bay leaves
- 5 dashes of Worcestershire sauce
- 1/2 cup fresh parsley
- To taste, add some coarse salt to the dish and freshly-ground black pepper

Instructions:

1. Combine the stew beef, vinegar, and water in a large saucepan. Bring to a boil on medium heat. Reduce heat to medium and simmer the stew beef mixture for approximately 1 1/2 hours, or until it is tender but not falling apart. You can check the meat now and again to ensure that the liquid is not evaporated. If necessary, add a little water. The juice should be concentrated with flavor.

2. Stews should be cooked at low temperatures. The liquid's surface should not move. The fat from rich meats will melt if you simmer the dish gently. Once the stew beef

has been cooked, add wine, tomato paste, beef stock, and bay leaves. Reduce heat to low and simmer for one hour, stirring frequently.

3. Cook the barley for 30 minutes more, stirring now and then. After checking that the barley has been cooked, remove it from the heat.

4. Add Worcestershire sauce and parsley to the bowl. Season with salt and pepper. Before serving, remove and discard bay leaves.

5. Keep it in a sealed container and freeze for up to a three months.

Nutritional Values Per Serving

Kcal	Fat	Carbs	Sugars	Fibers	Proteins	Salt
620	50 g	32 g	0 g	2 g	33 g	1.38 g

Preserving Beef Braised in Barolo Wine

Preparation Time: 20 minutes

Cooking Time: 3 hours

Ingredients For 6 Servings:

- 1 boneless beef-chuck roast (about 3 1/2 lbs), tied
- Sea salt, coarse salt, and freshly ground pepper
- 4 ounces pancetta cut into 1/2-inch cubes
- 2 medium onions, 1 medium chop
- 2 medium carrots, medium chop
- 2 medium celery stalks. Medium chop (use a potato peeler for the stringy parts)
- 1 tablespoon tomato paste
- Dice 3-4 garlic cloves
- 1/2 teaspoon sugar, granulated
- 1 tablespoon all-purpose flour, unbleached
- 1/2 of an Italian Barolo wine (750ml)
- 1 (14.5-ounce) can of diced tomatoes
- 3 Hatch chile peppers, blistered with skin and seed pods removed, chopped
- 1 sprig of fresh thyme and 1 teaspoon of minced leaves
- 1 small sprig of fresh rosemary
- 2 tablespoons chopped parsley leaves

Instructions:

1. Preheat the oven to 300°F.
2. Use paper towels to dry the beef. This is essential as any surface moisture can affect browning. As shown in the photo, tie the roast using cotton kitchen twine. Sprinkle salt and pepper all over.
3. Cook pancetta in a Dutch oven until crispy. Stir occasionally. Once the pancetta is crisp, transfer it to a Dutch oven and place it on a paper towel-lined plate.

4. Cook the chuck roast in the pot until browned on all sides. Transfer to a large plate; set aside.

5. Sauté the onion, carrots, and celery in the pot. Stir occasionally until the vegetables turn a golden brown. Add the sugar, flour, and crispy pancetta. Stir constantly until the mixture is well combined. To remove any browned bits from the bottom of your pan, add wine, chile peppers, and tomatoes. Add the rosemary sprig, thyme leaves, and sprig.

6. The browned chuck roast and any juices should be returned to the pot. Bring to a boil, then turn off the heat. Place in the oven and cover with a lid.

7. Use an oven-safe glove or tongs to turn the meat for 45 minutes per hour. Cook the beef until it is almost tender, about 3 hours.

8. Check the internal temperature of your beef after approximately three hours. Remove the meat from the oven when the internal temperature registers 180°F on the thermometer.

9. Once the meat has been cooked, take it out of the oven and transfer it to a cutting board. To keep the heart warm, cover it with aluminum foil and allow it to rest for approximately 15 minutes. This will allow juices to settle and cool down a bit.

10. Use a large, shallow spoon to scrape the fat from the surface of the braising sauce. Add the parsley leaves to the sauce.

11. Let the roast rest for at least 30 minutes. Slice the roast and serve it with the braising liquid or you freeze in the freezer for 3 weeks.

Nutritional Values Per Serving

Kcal	Fat	Carbs	Sugars	Fibers	Proteins	Salt
389	48 g	34 g	0 g	2 g	33 g	1.38 g

Preserving Beef Burgundy Stew

Preparation Time: 30 minutes

Cooking Time: 3 hours

Ingredients:

- 3 pounds beef meat (sirloin beef bottom round, rump roasted, chuck roast), boneless. Cut into 1-inch cubes
- 3 to 4 black peppercorns
- 1 (75 ml) Bottle of dry red wine
- 5 slices of bacon cut into 1/2-inch pieces
- 1 to 2 tablespoons olive or vegetable oils
- 2 cloves minced
- 1 medium onion, sliced
- 1 tablespoon freshly squeezed lemon juice

- 1 teaspoon Worcestershire Sauce
- 1 tablespoon tomato paste
- 2 bay leaves, dried
- To taste, add some coarse salt and freshly ground pepper
- 1 teaspoon of sugar (granulated)
- 1/8 teaspoon ground allspice/ground cloves
- 1/2 teaspoon paprika
- 1 to 3 cups beef broth or stock (homemade, store-bought), heat
- 6 carrots, peeled. Slice diagonally into 1-inch cubes
- 1 lb small white onions (pearl onion)
- 6 potatoes, cubes
- 1 lb mushrooms, stems removed and caps thickly sliced
- Parsley (for garnishment)
- *Baked egg noodles (optional)*
- *Thick crusty bread (optional)*

Instructions:

1. *The day before: Add the beef cubes, peppercorns, and wine to a large bowl. Wrap the bowl in plastic wrap and place it in the refrigerator for 24 hours.*

2. After 24 hours, take the beef out of the fridge and pour off the wine marinade. Use paper towels to dry the meat. Dry the meat thoroughly with paper towels before browning.

3. Cook bacon in considerable support or cast iron Dutch oven on medium heat until golden brown. Transfer bacon to a plate and let cool. Heat olive oil or vegetable oil in bacon fat until hot. Add marinated beef cubes to the skillet and cook until golden brown—transfer beef to a plate.

4. When you brown meat for stew, don't rush. This is an important step and should take between 10 and 15 minutes.

5. Don't crowd the pan with the meat. Only brown a little at a time. Leave space between each piece of beef, so it doesn't steam.

6. Sauté onion and garlic until soft. Add the red wine marinade, Worcestershire sauce, and tomato paste. Season with salt, pepper, sugar, allspice, cloves, and paprika. Add the bacon, browned beef cubes, and any accumulated juices. You will need to add enough hot beef broth/stock to cover the meat. Reduce heat to low and cover the heart. Continue to simmer for 2 to 3 hours, occasionally stirring until tender.

7. Stews should be cooked at low temperatures. The liquid's surface should not move. The fat from rich meats will melt if you simmer the dish gently. You can then chill the word and skim off any excess fat. To finish cooking, you can place the pot with the stew in an oven. At 325°F for 2 hours. Remove bay leaves and discard. Add carrots, onions, and potatoes. Continue to simmer for 30 minutes or until the meat and vegetables become tender.

8. Once the vegetables have been cooked, take them off the heat and place them in individual bowls.

9. Serve with potatoes, egg noodles, or in individual bowls. Garnish with parsley.

10. Keep it in a sealed container and freeze for up to a two months.

Nutritional Values Per Serving

Kcal	Fat	Carbs	Sugars	Fibers	Proteins	Salt
479	46 g	30 g	0 g	2 g	35 g	1.38 g

Meatball Soup

Preparation Time: 1 hour

Cooking Time: 1 hour

Ingredients:

- 1 box Onion Soup Mix
- 1 package Knorr Vegetable Soup Mix
- 1 large box of mixed vegetables, frozen (of choice)
- 1 can (10.5 ounces) cream of mushroom soup
- 1 can (14.5 ounces) tomato sauce
- 6 cups of water
- 1 handful of barley
- 1 teaspoon garlic powder
- Salt and pepper to your liking
- 1 1/2 lb ground turkey or ground beef lean (hamburgers)

Instructions:

1. Add the Onion Soup Mix to a large soup pan or Dutch oven on medium heat. Next, add water, barley, and garlic powder. Mix all ingredients until well combined. Seasoning packets contain a lot of salt and flavorings. Make sure to taste it before you add any more salt or spices.

2. Bring the soup to a boil. Reduce heat to medium-low.

3. Cut off about 1/2-inch chunks of raw hamburger, roll them into small balls and drop them into the soup. Let simmer for approximately 40-60 minutes.

4. Soup is ready when the hamburger balls have been cooked thoroughly, and the frozen vegetables are tender.

5. Make individual soup bowls. Serve with salad and sourdough bread.

6. Keep it in a sealed container and freeze for up to a three months.

Nutritional Values Per Serving

Kcal	Fat	Carbs	Sugars	Fibers	Proteins	Salt
529	45 g	34 g	0 g	2 g	36 g	1.38 g

Preserving Beef Stew and Parsley Dumplings

Preparation Time: 30 minutes

Cooking Time: 15 minutes

Ingredients For 6 Servings:

- Beef Stew
- 2 pounds Chin beef, or any other stewing animal
- 3 tablespoons (1 1/2 ounces) flour, season with salt and pepper
- 1/4 cup (2 ounces), beef dripping
- 2 medium onions chopped
- 2 cups (1 pint), beef stock
- 1 cup (1 1/2 pint) apple cider
- Salt a pinch
- Freshly-ground black pepper
- 1 cup (8 ounces), carrots, peeled & diced
- 1 cup (8 ounces), turnips, peeled & diced
- 2 sticks of celery, chopped and cleaned

- Parsley Dumplings
- 1/4 cup (2 ounces) flour (self-rising)
- 1/4 cup (2 ounces) fresh breadcrumbs
- 2 Tablespoons Suet, shredded
- 1 tablespoon chopped parsley
- 2 teaspoons finely grated lemon zest (rind)
- Salt a pinch
- Black pepper
- 1 egg, beaten

Instructions:

Beef Stew and Parsley Dumplings:

1. Slice the meat into 1-inch pieces and mix with the seasoned flour.
2. Heat the beef dripping in an oven-proof soup pan (or cast iron frying pan or Dutch oven). Sauté the onions until tender and translucent. Stir in the meat and fry to a golden brown.
3. Add the beef stock and cider to the saucepan. Scrape up any bits stuck to the pan— season with salt and pepper. Bring to a boil. Remove any white scum. Reduce heat to medium-low. Cover the pot with the turnips, celery, carrots, and celery. Let the stew simmer for about 2 hours, or until the meat is tender. *NOTE: To finish cooking, you can place the pot with the stew in an oven.* Cook at 325°F
4. Stews should be cooked at low temperatures. The liquid's surface should not move. Slowly simmer the stew until the fat is melted from rich meats. You can then chill the dish and skim off any excess fat.
5. Make the Parsley Dumplings (see above). Place the balls of dough on top of the stew. Cover with a lid and continue cooking for 15 to 20 more minutes. The dumplings should have about twice the size when done.

6. Place the stew, vegetables, and dumplings in a large bowl. Serve immediately with chunks of crusty bread.

Parsley Dumplings:

1. Combine the flour, breadcrumbs, and suet in a large bowl. Mix well with a spoon or fork. Season the mixture with salt and pepper. Mix in the beaten eggs.
2. Use a floured hand to form the dough into balls about the same size as large walnuts.
3. Keep it in a sealed container and freeze for up to four months.

Nutritional Values Per Serving

Kcal	Fat	Carbs	Sugars	Fibers	Proteins	Salt
509	48 g	34 g	0 g	2 g	33 g	1.38 g

Preserving Vegetable Beef Soup

Preparation Time: 30 minutes

Cooking Time: 2 hours

Ingredients For 10 Servings:

- 1 1/2 to 2 lb stew beef, chopped into bite-sized pieces
- To taste, add some coarse salt to the dish and freshly-ground black pepper
- 1 large onion, chopped and peeled
- 3-4 ribs celery, chopped
- 3-4 carrots, peeled
- 2 to 3 red potatoes chopped
- 2 tablespoons of olive oils, divided
- 3 cloves garlic, minced
- 2 cups fresh or frozen green beans
- 2 cans (14.5 ounces) of tomatoes with liquid, diced
- 1 1/2 teaspoons beef bouillon powder granules
- 1 (1.4-ounces) box of Knorr Vegetable Mix
- 1 tablespoon Worcestershire Sauce
- 2 bay leaves
- 2 32-ounce containers of beef stock or broth
- 2 bay leaves

Instructions:

1. Cut up beef and vegetables (celery and carrots, potatoes, etc.) into bite-sized pieces.
2. Cook the beef in a large stockpot on medium heat until it is browned on all sides. Salt and pepper to your liking. Place the browned beef on a plate.
3. Sauté celery and onions in olive oil for about 2 minutes, until translucent.
4. Mix the beef bouillon, vegetable soup, Worcestershire sauce, and garlic. Add the bay leaves. Mix everything and add enough beef stock to cover all the vegetables. Cook the soup until it boils.

5. Reduce the heat to low and allow the soup to simmer for approximately 1 1/2 to 2 hours, or until the potatoes and carrots are tender. If necessary, season the soup with salt and pepper.

6. Serve in bowls, and enjoy! Or store in the refridgerator for 2 weeks.

Nutritional Values Per Serving

Kcal	Fat	Carbs	Sugars	Fibers	Proteins	Salt
689	48 g	34 g	0 g	2 g	33 g	1.38 g

Preserving Gourmet Roast Beef Sandwich

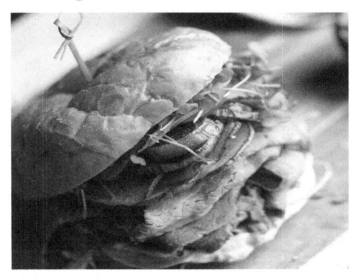

Preparation Time: 10 minutes

Cooking Time: 5 minutes

Ingredients For 5 Servings:

- 1 loaf of crusty Italian bread

- Dijon mustard
- 1 lb deli roast beef (cooked medium to rare)
- Salt to taste
- Black peppercorns, coarsely ground
- Provolone cheese, sliced
- Red onion, sliced
- Sliced kosher dill pickles
- Washed and trimmed Arugula leaves

Instructions:

1. Split bread loaves horizontally. Take out any excess bread and leave about 1-inch between the sides and bottom.
2. Use Dijon mustard to coat both halves of the bread.
3. Begin by building the sandwich using roast beef. Next, add Provolone cheese and red onion. Finally, garnish with arugula leaves.
4. Place the top on and cut into individual portions.
5. Keep it in a sealed container and freeze for up to two months.

Nutritional Values Per Serving

Kcal	Fat	Carbs	Sugars	Fibers	Proteins	Salt
689	48 g	34 g	0 g	2 g	33 g	1.38 g

Preserving Pork Chops With Mushroom Cream Sauce

Preparation Time: 10 minutes

Cooking Time: 20 minutes

Ingredients For 4 Servings:

- 4 bone in pork chops 1 1/2" thick
- 2 tbsp olive oil
- 1 teaspoon salt
- Freshly ground pepper
- 6 tbsp butter
- 2 lbs crimini mushrooms, with the tough ends removed and cut in half
- 3 garlic cloves, minced
- 1 cup dry white wine
- 1 cup heavy cream
- 1 tbsp dijon mustard
- 2 Tbsp Fresh Thyme, minced

- 1lemon
- 2 tbsp fresh chives

Instructions:

1. Use a paper towel to dry the pork chops. Salt and pepper the meat.
2. Heat oil in a large skillet with a heavy bottom until it smokes. Set two pork chops at once in the pan. Flip the pork chops after 3 minutes. Continue cooking for 3 more minutes. Flip the chops until they reach 160 degrees F. Keep going with the rest of the pork chops.
3. Turn down heat to medium, and then add butter to the saucepan. Stir in the mushrooms once they have melted. Continue stirring until the mushrooms are cooked through.
4. Cook for one more minute.
5. Place the wine and the fresh thyme in a saucepan. Bring to a boil. Let the mushroom mixture simmer for at least half an hour.
6. Mix in the heavy cream and mustard. Stir until everything is well combined.
7. Season with salt and pepper. Add the pork chops to the skillet and pour the sauce over them.
8. Serve the dish with fresh lemon juice and chives. Serve the dish warm with lots of sauce and mushrooms
9. Keep it in a sealed container and freeze for up to a one month

Nutritional Values Per Serving

Calories	Cholesterol	Fat	Carbs	Sugars	Fibers	Proteins	Sodium
538	128 mg	37 g	13 g	5 g	2 g	30 g	761 mg

Preserving Grilled Pork Tenderloin With Chimichurri

Preparation Time: 10 minutes

Cooking Time: 20 minutes

Ingredients For 10 Servings:

- 2.5 lb pork tenderloin. Fat trimmed
- 1 Tbsp brown sugar
- 1 Tbsp kosher salt
- 1 Tbsp paprika
- 2 tsp freshly cracked black Pepper
- 1 Tbsp Garlic Powder
- 1 cup homemade chimichurri sauce
- vegetable oil (olive, grapeseed, avocado)

Instructions:

1. Combine the brown sugar, salt, and paprika in a bowl.

2. The seasoning should be mixed with the tenderloin until it is evenly coated.

To bake the tenderloin:

1. Pre-heat oven to 400°F. Place the rack in the middle.

2. Heat 1-2 tablespoons of oil in a large cast-iron or ovenproof skillet on medium heat. Cook the tenderloin in the pan until evenly browned (about 5-6 minutes).

3. Bake the pan for 15 minutes more in the oven, flipping halfway through. Bake the meat until it reaches 145 degrees F.

4. Transfer the pork onto a cutting board. Let it rest for at most three minutes.

5. Slice and serve or Keep it in a freezing bagand freeze for up to three months.

Nutritional Values Per Serving

Calories	Cholesterol	Fat	Carbs	Sugars	Fibers	Proteins	Sodium
217	67 mg	13 g	4 g	1 g	0 g	20 g	465 mg

Preserving Hoisin Pork Served With Garlic & Ginger Leaves

Preparation Time: 10 minutes

Cooking Time: 10 minutes

Ingredients:

- 500 g pork loin steak, cut into slices of 2cm thickness
- 4 tbsp hoisin sauce
- 1 tbsp light sauce, plus a dash
- 350 g thin-stemmed broccoli
- 1 tbsp sunflower oils
- 2 cloves of garlic, thinly sliced
- 5 cm-piece ginger, shredded
- 1 bunch of spring onions, cut in half lengthways
- 350 g Bok Choi, cut in half lengthways
- *Rice or noodles to be served (optional)*

Instructions:

1. Place the pork, hoisin, and soy sauce into a bowl. Let stand for 10 minutes. Turn the grill on high and shake off the excess sauce. Then, place the pork on a plate. Turn the pork halfway through cooking—grill for 5 minutes. Leave to cool in a warm area for 5 minutes.

2. In the meantime, place the broccoli in a microwave-safe bowl and add 4 tbsp of water. Cover with cling foil, then microwave for 3 minutes on High. Stir-fry the ginger and garlic for one minute in olive oil. Stir-fry the spring onions, bok choi, and for 2 more minutes. Stir-fry the broccoli for another 2 minutes until it is tender. If you wish, serve the pork with the greens and a drizzle of any remaining pork juices.

3. Keep it in a Freezing bagand freeze for up to a two months

Nutritional Values Per Serving

Kcal	Fat	Carbs	Sugars	Fibers	Proteins	Salt
420	28 g	12 g	8 g	6 g	31 g	1.5 g

Home Preseerved Healthy Beef Chow Meal

Preparation Time: 10 minutes

Cooking Time: 10 minutes

Ingredients:

- 2 wholemeal noodles nests (85 g)
- 2 tsp sesame or rapeseed oil
- 200 g lean fillet steak. Fat removed. Cut into strips
- 1 small red onion (100g), finely chopped
- 11.5 g ginger pieces, peeled and finely chopped
- 160 g of chestnut mushrooms, thinly sliced
- 2 cloves of garlic, chopped fine
- 160 g ready-to-eat beansprouts
- 1 1/2 tsp tamari
- 1 tbsp brown Rice Vinegar
- 4 spring onions (65 g), chopped into diagonal lengths

Instructions:

1. Follow the package instructions to cook the noodles—heat half of the oil in a large wok. Once the noodles are cooked, stir-fry the beef for 30 seconds on high heat until browned. Transfer the meat to a plate and set it aside. The remaining oil can be added to the wok. Stir fry the ginger and onion until softened. To prevent burning, add a little water and cover the pan for 2 to 3 minutes.

2. Stir in the garlic and mushrooms, and fry for 3 minutes. Add the beansprouts to the pan and cook for another minute until the beans are hot.

3. Combine the vinegar and tamari with 2 tbsp water in a small bowl. Toss the noodles with the vinegar and 2 tbsp water in a bowl. Next, add the tamari mixture, spring onion, and beef to the wok. Stir fry for a few more minutes to heat through. Add plenty of black pepper to the mix and stir-fry until well combined.

4. Keep it in a freezing bagand freeze for up to three months.

Nutritional Values Per Serving

Kcal	Fat	Carbs	Sugars	Fibers	Proteins	Salt
407	11 g	41 g	10 g	8 g	32 g	1 g

Preserving Rump Steak with Mushroom and Red Wine Sauce

Preparation Time: 5 minutes

Cooking Time: 10 minutes

Ingredients For 2 Servings:

- 1 tbsp sunflower oils
- 2 rump steaks (about 200 g/8oz each)
- 140 g mushrooms, quartered
- 2 Thyme sprigs. Leaves removed
- Red wine 150 ml
- 1 tbsp butter

Instructions:

1. In a large skillet, heat the oil. Season the steaks and fry them for 2 to 3 minutes on each side for medium-rare. You can cook it longer if you prefer. Take the steaks out of the pan and let them rest in a bowl.

2. Cook the mushrooms and the thyme leaves in the pan for about a minute or until they are softened and golden. Turn off the heat, add the wine, and let it bubble until the butter is melted. Season.

3. Serve the steaks with mushroom sauce, creamy mash, and some spring greens.

4. Keep it in a sealed container and freeze for up to four months.

Nutritional Values Per Serving

Kcal	Fat	Carbs	Sugars	Fibers	Proteins	Salt
500	32 g	4 g	4 g	1 g	43 g	0.42 g

Preserving Garlic Lamb With Peppers and Couscous

Preparation Time: 5 minutes

Cooking Time: 10 minutes

Ingredients For 2 Servings:

- 2 x packets of plain or flavored couscous
- 50 g homemade or purchased garlic butter
- 2 tbsp olive oil
- 4 lamb leg steaks
- 250 g roasted pepper strips purchased from the deli or 285 g jar-roasted pepper strips
- 20 Kalamata olives
- A handful of mint or flatleaf Parsley
- 1 lemon
- 4 tbsp toasted flaked nuts

Instructions:

1. Turn the kettle on and place both couscous packets in a heatproof bowl. In a large frying pan, heat the garlic butter on medium heat. Add a tablespoon of oil—Fry the lamb steaks for 4 minutes on each side. Stir in 400ml/14fl Oz boiling water and pour over the couscous. Allow to cool, then add the oil.

2. Add the olives and peppers to the pan along with the lamb. Add the chopped herbs to the pan and cook until the lamb is done—season with the lemon juice.

3. Add the almonds to the couscous, and then spoon it onto serving plates. Serve the couscous with the lamb, peppers, and olives.

4. Keep it in a sealed container and freeze for up to three months.

Nutritional Values Per Serving

Kcal	Fat	Carbs	Sugars	Fibers	Proteins	Salt
689	48 g	34 g	0 g	2 g	33 g	1.38 g

Preserving Steak Marinade

Preparation Time: 5 minutes

Cooking Time: 5 minutes

Ingredients For 4 Servings:

- 1/2 cup olive oil, extra-virgin
- 1/3 cup soy sauce
- 1/4 cup balsamic vinegar
- 1/4 cup Worcestershire sauce
- 1/3 cup fresh-squeezed lemon juice
- Finely mince 3 garlic cloves
- 2 teaspoons brown sugar
- 1 cup chopped fresh basil
- 1/4 cup chopped fresh parsley
- 1 teaspoon of white pepper

- 1/8 teaspoon cayenne pepper
- Salt to your taste

Instructions:

1. Combine the olive oil, balsamic vinegar, and Worcestershire sauce in a medium bowl. Add the garlic, ginger, garlic, brown sugar, and salt. Mix well.
2. Seal the steak with the marinade. Marinating meat should be kept in the refrigerator for a minimum of 2 hours
3. Keep any leftover barbecue sauce in an airtight container. Refrigerate for up to two weeks.

Nutritional Values Per Serving

Kcal	Fat	Carbs	Sugars	Fibers	Proteins	Salt
430	58 g	31 g	0 g	2 g	35 g	1.38 g

POULTRY

Preserving Chicken Curry

Preparation Time: 5 minutes

Cooking Time: 45 minutes

Ingredients For 4 Servings:

- 2 tbsp sunflower oils
- 1 onion, thinly chopped
- 2 crushed garlic cloves
- A thumb-sized chunk of grated ginger
- 6 chicken thighs, boneless & skinless
- 3 Tbsp medium spice paste (tikka works great)
- 400 g can chopped tomatoes
- 100 g Greek yogurt
- 1 small bunch of coriander leaves, chopped
- 50 g ground almonds
- Bread and cooked basmati rice to serve

Instructions:

1. Place the oil in a large saucepan or flameproof casserole dish—heat on medium heat. Stir in the onion with a pinch of salt. Fry for 8-10 minutes, or until golden brown and sticky. Cook for another minute.

2. Cut the chicken into 3cm chunks, then add it to the pan—Fry for 5 minutes before adding the spice paste, tomatoes, and 250ml water. Bring to a boil. Reduce heat to low and simmer. Cover and cook for about 25-30 minutes or until the sauce is thickened and reduced—season with yogurt, coriander, and ground almonds. You can either eat it right away or let it cool in a freezer bag for up to two months. Serve with fluffy Basmati rice.

Nutritional Values Per Serving

Kcal	Fat	Saturated	Carbs
354	23 g	4 g	10 g

Sugars	Fibers	Proteins	Salt
8 g	3 g	24 g	0.6 g

Preserving Chicken fajitas

Preparation Time: 15 minutes

Cooking Time: 10 minutes

Ingredients For 3 Servings:

- 2 large, sliced chicken breasts
- 1 finely chopped red onion
- 1 red bell pepper, sliced
- *1 red chili, finely chopped (optional)*

Marinade:

- 1 heaped tablespoon smoked paprika
- Ground coriander: 1 tbsp
- 1 teaspoon ground cumin

- 2 medium garlic cloves, crushed
- 4 tbsp olive oil
- 1 lime, juiced
- Tabasco - 4-5 drops

For serving:

- 6 medium tortillas
- bag mixed salad
- Fresh salsa in a 230g tub

Instructions:

1. Place 6 tortillas in foil and heat oven to 200C/180C fan/gas 6.
2. Combine 1 heaped tablespoon smoked paprika, 1 teaspoon ground coriander, 2 crushed garlic cloves, and 4 tbsp of olive oil with the juice of 1 lime. Add 4-5 drops of Tabasco to taste. Mix all ingredients in a large bowl—season with salt and pepper.
3. In the marinade, stir 2 thinly sliced chicken breasts and 1 finely chopped red onion, 1 finely diced red pepper, and 1 finely cut red chili, if desired.
4. Place the chicken on a griddle plate and heat until it is hot.
5. Heat everything on high for 5 minutes to achieve a nice charred look. You may need to make two batches if your griddle pan is small.
6. Check the chicken's doneness by tearing off the thickest portion.
7. To heat the tortillas, place them in the oven. Serve with cooked chicken, a bag of mixed salad, and one 230g container of fresh salsa. You can also cool the tortillas and freeze them in appropriate batches for 3 months.

Nutritional Values Per Serving

Kcal	Fat	Saturated	Carbs
723	26 g	6 g	77 g

Sugars	Fibers	Proteins	Salt
12 g	11 g	39 g	2.48 g

Preserving Piri-Piri Chicken Served With Smashed Sweet Potatoes and Broccoli

Preparation Time: 20 minutes

Cooking Time: 55 minutes

Ingredients For 4 Servings:

- 3 large sweet potatoes (approximately 900 g), peeled and chopped into large pieces
- Oil for drizzling
- 6-8 chicken breasts, skin left on
- 2 red onions, cut into wedges
- 25 g sachet of Piri-Piri spice mixture (or a milder version, if desired)
- 300 g long-stem broccoli

Instructions:

1. The oven should be heated to 180C/160C fan/gas 4. Add the sweet potatoes to a large bowl and drizzle with oil. Season the dish with salt and pepper. Place the sweet potatoes on one side of the baking tin. Next, add the onion, spice mixture, oil, and seasoning to the chicken. Turn everything halfway through—roast for 40 minutes. Toss the broccoli in the tin.

2. Take the chicken, onion, and broccoli out of the tin. Use a fork to mash the potatoes, including all the spices and chicken juices from the pan. Spread the mash on the bottom of the can. Next, add the onions, broccoli, and chicken to the top. Finally, place the container in the middle of the table and enjoy or freeze them in appropriate batches for 6 months.

Nutritional Values Per Serving

Kcal	Fat	Saturated	Carbs
662	23 g	6 g	74 g

Sugars	Fibers	Proteins	Salt
40 g	15 g	32 g	2.1 g

Preserving Simple Chicken Tagine

Preparation Time: 10 minutes

Cooking Tme: 40 minutes

Ingredients For 4 Servings:

- 2 tbsp olive oil
- 8 skinless, boneless chicken thighs
- 1 onion chopped

- 2 tsp grated fresh ginger root

- 1 teaspoon saffron, turmeric

- 400 g carrot, cut into sticks

- Small bunch of parsley, roughly chopped

- Lemon wedges, to be served

Instructions:

1. In a large pan, heat the oil. Add the chicken and fry until it is lightly colored. Stir in the ginger and onion, then cook for 2 minutes more.

2. Season the mixture with 150ml water, honey, and carrots. Stir well. Bring to a boil. Cover and simmer for 30 minutes until the chicken is tender. Remove the cover and heat the pan for 5 minutes to reduce the sauce slightly. Sprinkle the seasoning with parsley. Serve with lemon wedges. Cool it and freeze it in portions for up to two months.

Nutritional Values Per Serving

Kcal	Fat	Saturated	Carbs
304	11 g	3 g	14 g

Sugars	Fibers	Proteins	Salt
12 g	3 g	39 g	0.48 g

Preserving Easy Chicken Kiev

Preparation Time: 15 minutes

Cooking Time: 25 minutes

Ingredients For 4 Servings:

- 6 cloves of garlic, 2 peeled
- small bunch of flat-leaf parsley
- 85 g fresh breadcrumbs
- 4 skinless, boneless chicken breasts
- 4 tbsp garlic and soft herb cheese
- 4 tsp olive oil

Instructions:

1. The oven should be at 200C/180C fan/gas 6. Combine the parsley, 2 garlic cloves, and 1 tablespoon of olive oil in a food processor. Mix in the breadcrumbs and seasoning. Tip onto a plate.

2. At the plump side of each chicken breast, cut a small slit. To seal, place a quarter of the soft cheese into each hole. After brushing the oil on the chicken breasts, apply the herby crumbs to them.

3. Place the chicken coated in a shallow baking tin. Sprinkle the remaining garlic cloves unpeeled on the chicken and drizzle the remaining oil. Bake the chicken for about 20-25 minutes, or until it is cooked through and the crumbs are crisp and golden. You can either serve the chicken with the soft-roasted garlic skins or let it cool in a freezer bag for up to four months.

Nutritional Values Per Serving

Kcal	Fat	Saturated	Carbs
327	12 g	5 g	18 g

Sugars	Fibers	Proteins	Salt
1 g	1 g	38 g	0.8 g

Preserving Easy Chicken Stir-Fry

Preparation Time: 15 minutes

Cooking Time: 20 minutes + 15 minutes marinating

Ingredients For 4 Servings:

- 4 skinless, boneless chicken breast fillets
- 1 egg white
- 1 tbsp cornflour, plus 1 tsp extra
- 350 g fragrant Thai rice
- Root ginger knob about thumb-sized
- 1 shallot
- 1 clove of garlic
- 1 tbsp vegetable oils
- 1 tbsp fish sauce
- Juice 1 lime
- A handful of basil leaves
- *Optional: 1 red chili*

Instructions:

1. You can Velvet the chicken by cutting the chicken into small pieces. In a bowl, beat together the egg whites and 1 tbsp cornflour. Mix the egg white and 1 tbsp cornflour in a bowl. Add the chicken to the mixture. Marinate the chicken for between 15-30 minutes. Please do not place the mixture in the refrigerator, as it will harden. Rinse the rice under cold water until it runs clear.

2. Perfect rice is made by draining it and placing it in a saucepan with a lid. Pour 600ml of water and sprinkle with salt. The water should boil. Once the water is boiling, let the rice simmer covered for about 10 minutes or until it becomes translucent and tiny craters form. Cover the rice with a lid and continue cooking for another 10 minutes.

3. Get the ingredients ready. Take a teaspoon of ginger skin and cut it into small pieces. Cut the stalk and inner pith off the pepper. Divide the pepper into bite-sized pieces. Slice the garlic clove and shallot into thin slices. If you prefer the chili milder, trim the ends. Let the chicken drain the egg marinade from the bowl and dry it on kitchen paper.

4. Stir-frying is foolproof: Heat 1 tablespoon of oil in a large saucepan. Toss the chicken in oil for 7-10 minutes. Set aside. If necessary, add more oil. Cook the pepper for 1 minute, then add the shallot, ginger, and garlic and cook for another 1-2 minutes. Mix the fish sauce, lime juice, and 50ml water with 1 teaspoon cornflour. Place the chicken in the wok. Cook the chicken for about 1 minute, then stir in the basil. Serve with rice, let cool down and freeze the leftovers in separate containers for five months.

Kcal	Fat	Saturated	Carbs
501	5 g	1 g	76 g

Sugars	Fibers	Proteins	Salt
3 g	2 g	42 g	1.02 g

Preserving Crockpot Chicken Taco Meat

Preparation Time: 5 minutes

Cooking Time: 2 hours

Ingredients For 8 Servings:

- 112 oz red salsa tub, preferably from the refrigerated area
- 1.5 lb boneless, skinless chicken breast

- 1/4 cup homemade taco seasoning or 1 packet store-bought

Instructions:

1. All ingredients in a Crock-Pot.
2. Cover and cook on low for four hours or high for two hours.
3. Chop the chicken and add it to the juices.
4. Serve meat with your favorite tacos or salad fixings
5. All ingredients into a freezer bag. Seal the bag to remove as much air as possible. You can freeze the mixture for up to six months.

Nutritional Values Per Serving

Kcal	Fat	Carbs	Sugars	Fibers
175	6 g	3 g	1 g	0 g

Proteins	Salt	Cholesterol	Sodium
25 g	0.42 g	76 mg	366 mg

Preserving Mango Chutney Chicken

Preparation Time: 10 minutes

Cooking Time: 45 minutes

Ingredients For 6 Servings:

- 8 boneless, skinless chicken thighs, approximately 2 lbs
- 1 (9 oz) jar mango chutney
- 1 head of cauliflower cut into florets
- 3 tbsp olive oils
- 2 teaspoons salt
- For serving, you can use cooked rice, quinoa, or couscous
- *Optional: chopped cilantro*
  Red onion, thinly chopped

Instructions:

1. Preheat the oven to 375°F. Place cauliflower on a baking sheet. Toss in olive oil, 1 teaspoon salt, and 2 tablespoons of water—Cook for 20 minutes. Take out of the oven.

2. Toss the chicken thighs in a large bowl with 1 teaspoon of salt and chutney—the place between half-cooked cauliflower. Serve the chicken with any remaining chutney.

3. Bake the sheet pan for 25 minutes more, or until the chicken, is done and the cauliflower is crisp. Broil 5 minutes for crispy chicken

4. Add cilantro and thinly sliced red onions. Serve over cooked rice, quinoa, or couscous.

5. Keep it in a sealed container and freeze for up to five months.

Nutritional Values Per Serving

Kcal	Fat	Carbs	Sugars	Fibers
360	13 g	30 g	2 g	2 g

Proteins	Salt	Cholesterol	Sodium
31 g	0.42 g	140 mg	938 mg

Preserving Lemon Chicken

Preparation Time: 5 minutes

Cooking Time: 30 minutes

Ingredients For 6 Servings:

- 4 boneless chicken breasts (roughly 2.5 pounds)
- 1/4 cup olive oil
- 2 tsp oregano, dried
- 2 tsp thyme, dried
- 2 teaspoons Garlic Powder
- 2 teaspoons salt, divided
- 1/2 tsp black pepper
- 1/2 cup dry white wine such as Sauvignon Blanc or Pinot Grigio
- 2 tbsp minced garlic (6 cloves)
- 1 tbsp lemon zest (2 lemons)
- 2 tbsp lemon juice, freshly squeezed

- 1 tbsp brown sugar
- *Optional: 1 lemon, cut into 6 pieces*

Instructions:

1. The oven should be heated to 400°F.
2. Place the breasts of the chicken in a baking dish 9x13.
3. Mix the olive oil, garlic powder, olive oil, and thyme in a small bowl. Add 1 teaspoon salt to make a thick paste/marinade. Season the chicken breasts with seasoning paste.
4. Combine the white wine, garlic, and lemon zest with the lemon juice in a bowl. Add the brown sugar. Serve chicken breasts with the sauce.
5. Bake the chicken for 15 minutes. Then, place the lemon slices in between the chicken.
6. Keep it in a sealed container and freeze for up to three months.

Nutritional Values Per Serving

Kcal	Fat	Carbs	Sugars	Fibers
327	6 g	4 g	2 g	0 g

Proteins	Salt	Cholesterol	Sodium
40 g	0.42 g	0 mg	776 mg

Preserving Caesar Salad, Roast Chicken & Bacon

Preparation Time: 5 minutes

Cooking Time: 20 minutes

Ingredients For 3 Servings:

- 4 chicken breasts, skin on
- 8 slices of streaky bacon
- 1 clove of garlic, crushed
- Juice 1/2 lemon
- 3 tbsp natural yogurt
- 3 tbsp olive oil
- 50 g Parmesan, plus additional to serve
- 2 small romaine leaves
- *Worcestershire sauce (optional)*

Instructions:

1. Preheat oven to 200C/180C fan/gas 6. Season the chicken, and then place it in a small roasting pan. Place the bacon on top of the chicken. Roast for about 15-20 minutes, or until crispy and the chicken is cooked through.

2. Mix the yogurt, Parmesan, oil, lemon juice, yogurt, and oil. If you have Worcestershire sauce in your cupboard, add a Worcestershire sauce pinch. The outer leaves of the lettuce should be thrown away. Place the remaining lettuce on a plate and mix the dressing gently. Serve the chicken with crisp bacon and sprinkle extra Parmesan if desired.

3. Portion it in a sealed container and freeze for up to two months.

Nutritional Values Per Serving

Kcal	Fat	Carbs	Sugars	Fibers	Proteins	Salt
480	29 g	2 g	2 g	0 g	53 g	1.65 g

Preserving Butter Chicken

Preparation Time: 15 minutes

Cooking Time: 35 minutes + at least 1 hour marinating

Ingredients For 4 Servings:

- 500 g skinless boneless chicken thighs

For the marinade:

- 1 lemon, juiced
- 2 tsp ground cumin
- 2 tsp paprika
- 1-2 tsp hot chilli powder
- 200 g natural yogurt

For the curry:

- 2 tbsp vegetable oil
- 1 large onion, chopped
- 3 garlic cloves, crushed
- thumb-sized piece ginger, grated
- 1 tsp garam masala
- 2 tsp ground fenugreek
- 3 tbsp tomato purée
- 300 ml chicken stock
- 50 g flaked almonds, toasted
- *1 green chilli, deseeded and finely chopped (optional)*

To serve (optional):

- cooked basmati rice
- naan bread
- mango chutney or lime pickle
- fresh coriander
- lime wedges

Instructions:

1. Heat a large skillet or medium saucepan over medium-high heat. Add the oil, butter, and onions and cook onions down until lightly golden, about 3-4 minutes. Add ginger and garlic and let cook for 30 seconds, stirring so it doesn't burn.
2. Add the chicken, tomato paste, and spices. Cook for 5-6 minutes or until everything is cooked through.
3. Add the heavy cream and simmer for 8-10 minutes stirring occasionally. Serve over Basmati rice or with naan.
4. Portion butter chicken in a sealed container and freeze for up to six weeks.

Nutritional Values Per Serving

Kcal	Fat	Saturated	Carbs
367	18 g	3 g	12 g

Sugars	Fibers	Proteins	Salt
10 g	3 g	37 g	0.6 g

Preserving Easy Teriyaki Chicken

Preparation Time: 5 minutes

Cooking Time: 15 minutes

Ingredients For 4 Servings:

- 2 tbsp toasted sesame oil
- 6 skinless and boneless chicken thighs, sliced
- 2 large garlic cloves, crushed
- 1 thumb-sized piece ginger, grated
- 50 g runny honey
- 30 ml light soy sauce
- 1 tbsp rice wine vinegar
- 1 tbsp sesame seeds , to serve
- 4 spring onions, shredded, to serve
- sticky rice, to serve
- steamed bok choi or spring greens, to serve

Instructions:

1. Heat the oil in a non-stick pan over a medium heat. Add the chicken and fry for 7 mins, or until golden. Add the garlic and ginger and fry for 2 mins. Stir in the honey, soy sauce, vinegar and 100ml water. Bring to the boil and cook for 2 - 5 mins over a medium heat until the chicken is sticky and coated in a thick sauce.

2. Scatter over the spring onions and sesame seeds, then serve the chicken with the rice and steamed veg.

3. Portion it in a sealed container and freeze for up to three months.

Nutritional Values Per Serving

Kcal	Fat	Saturated	Carbs
243	14 g	3 g	11 g

Sugars	Fibers	Proteins	Salt
11 g	1 g	18 g	1.23 g

SEAFOOD

Bonito Fish Preserved In Oil

Preparation Time: 1 hour and 20 minutes

Cooking Time: 10 minutes

Ingredients For 4 Servings:

- Bay leaves
- fish (fresh bonito, cut into pieces)
- Water
- Salt
- olive oil

Instructions:

1. Use the bay leaves to cover the bottom of large saucepans. Add the fish pieces and layer with water. Salt, 85-95 grams for each liter.

2. Add more bay leaves to the saucepan and let it simmer for 20-30 minutes. Let cool off the heat.

3. Take the fish out of the water. Then, remove the skin and bones.

4. You can sterilize canning jars with a 30-minute boil and then dry them upside down on a cloth.

5. Place the fish in rectangular pieces. Olive oil should be used to fill the jars.

6. Boil the canning jars for 30 minutes until they are sealed. Allow cooling.

7. Freeze it in the freezer for up for up to a year.

Nutritional Values Per Serving

Kcal	Fat	Saturated	Carbs
354	23 g	4 g	10 g

Sugars	Fibers	Proteins	Salt
8 g	3 g	24 g	0.6 g

Preserved Fish Rolls

Preparation Time: 40 minutes

Ingredients:

- 8 herring
- 1 cup salt
- 1 pinch sugar
- 2 cups white wine vinegar
- 1 1/3 cups water
- 1 1/8 cups sugar
- 14 allspice (crushed)
- Crushed 14 black peppercorns
- 3 bay Leaves
- 2 lemons (finely pared rind).
- 3 chives (snipped)

Kitchen utensils:

- 1 saucepan
- 1 skillet
- 1 small plate
- 1 bowl
- 1 cutting board
- 1 large knife
- 1 small blade
- 1 tablespoon
- 1 wooden spoon
- 1 sieve

Instructions:

1. Place the herring fillets into a baking dish. Combine the salt and sugar in a bowl. Cover the fish with this mixture. Cover the fish and let it chill for 24 hours.
2. The oven should be heated to 220°C (200° fan) or 425°F gas 7.
3. Combine the sugar, vinegar, water, and spices in a saucepan. Stir the mixture until the sugar is dissolved.
4. Remove the salt from the herring and discard it. Bring the fish to boil in the saucepan. Take the pan off the heat and add the lemon zest. Pour the contents into a baking dish.
5. Cover and cook for 20 minutes. Let cool. Then, let it cool. The bay leaves and spices should be thrown out.
6. Place the herring and liquid in cold, sterilized jars. Make sure that the fish is fully covered. Add the chopped chives to your jars. Seal the jars tightly. Keep in the refrigerator for up to 6 months.

Nutritional Values Per Serving

Kcal	Fat	Saturated	Carbs
354	23 g	4 g	10 g

Sugars	Fibers	Proteins	Salt
8 g	3 g	30 g	0.6 g

Salted Fish

Preparation Time: 40 minutes

Ready in: 2 days and 6 hours

Ingredients:

- Cod, haddock, and flounder fillets
- Kosher sea salt or medium-grain

Instructions:

1. Rinse the fish with water and dry it using a dishcloth. In a container, spread a layer of salt about 1/2 inch thick. Place pieces of fish on top of the salt, so they are not touching. Add another layer of salt to the fish pieces. Continue to alternate salt and fish layers until you have buried all fish in salt. Finish by adding at least 1/2 inch of salt.

2. For 2 days, place the salted fish in a cold cellar or refrigerator at 40 degrees Fahrenheit.

3. After two days, scrub the fish with as much salt as possible. Don't worry if it doesn't get rid of every speck. Wrap the fish in cheesecloth. Place the fish on a rack placed over a plate or tray. After a week, put it in a cold cellar or refrigerator.

4. Take out the cheesecloth. Store the salted fish in an airtight container in a fridge or cold cellar for up to a year.

5. If you are using salted fish, make sure to soak it for at least 24 hours and then change the water twice. It will taste even better if you drink it with frequent water changes for two days.

Nutritional Values Per Serving

Kcal	Fat	Saturated	Carbs	Sugars
276	13.8 g	8 g	11 g	0.1 g

Fibers	Proteins	Cholesterol	Sodium
3.1 g	27.8 g	94.6 g	215.8 mg

Preserving Prawn And Quinoa Salad

Preparation Time: 15 minutes

Cooking Time: 15 minutes

Ingredients For 2 Servings:

For the salad:

- 60 g quinoa
- 150 g shelled cooked prawns
- 1 small avocado, stoned and sliced
- 1/4 cucumber, halved and sliced
- 50 g watercress
- 100 g cherry tomatoes, halved

For the dressing:

- Finely grated zest and juice of 1 large lime

- 1 red chili - deseeded, finely chopped
- 2 spring onions, finely chopped and trimmed
- 1 tsp wheat-free tamari
- handful coriander, chopped
- 1 tsp Rapeseed Oil
- 1/2 tsp maple syrup

Instructions:

1. Boil the quinoa for 15 minutes in a small saucepan until they are tender and appear to have burst. Drain the quinoa well and place it in a bowl. In the meantime, prepare the dressing by mixing the lime zest and juice with the chili in the bowl.

2. Mix half of the dressing with the spring onions, tamari, and coriander. Mix all salad ingredients and spoon onto two plates.

3. Mix the remaining dressing with the oil and maple syrup and add the prawns. Spread the sauce on the quinoa salad. Sprinkle the coriander over the top.

4. Keep it in a sealed container and freeze for up to three months.

Nutritional Values Per Serving

Kcal	Fat	Saturated	Carbs
305	14 g	2 g	22 g

Sugars	Fibers	Proteins	Salt
7 g	7 g	19 g	1.5 g

Preserving Shrimps and Sausage

Preparation Time: 15 minutes

Cooking Time: 18 minutes

Ingredients For 6 Servings:

- 1 large, raw shrimp, peeled, deveined, tail on
- 1 lb chicken sausage, fully cooked
- 1 lb asparagus, trimmed into 3" pieces
- 2 medium shallots, cut into wedges
- 1 tbsp extra virgin oil
- 1 teaspoon salt
- 2 tsp old bay seasoning
- 1 lemon

To taste:

- pepper
- Lemon Garlic Aioli
- 1 cup of different light tasting olive oil
- 1egg
- 1garlic clove, mashed
- 1 lemon, 1 zest
- 1 Tbsp fresh lemon juice, starting at 1 lemon
- 1 teaspoon salt

Instructions:

1. Make the aioli by adding the olive oil, egg yolk, lemon juice, zest, and salt to a mason container. Turn on the immersion blender or hand blender and place it at the bottom. Within seconds, the aioli will begin to form at its base. The oil will rapidly emulsify, and it will become thick. Keep the blender in the bottom of your jar for a few seconds to ensure that the oil is fully incorporated. Then, move the blender slowly up until it is thoroughly combined.

2. To heat the oven, heat to 400F

3. Toss the asparagus and shallots with olive oil and 1/2 teaspoon salt in a large bowl. Spread on a baking sheet with the sausage—roast for 10 minutes on the center rack.

4. Add shrimp to the pan. Sprinkle remaining salt, fresh ground pepper, and old bay seasoning on the sheet pan. Finally, squeeze the lemon over it. Toss the ingredients in a pan. Roast for another 6-7 minutes, or until the sausage and the shrimp are pink. Serve warm with the aioli Enjoy!

5. Portion it in a sealed container and freeze for up to 8 weeks.

Nutritional Values Per Serving

Kcal	Fat	Cholesterol	Carbs
596	51 g	212 mg	13 g

Sugars	Fibers	Proteins	Sodium
6 g	3 g	24 g	1966 mg

Preserving Baked Salmon With Grapefruit Salad

Preparation Time: 15 minutes

Cooking Time: 15 minutes

Ingredients For 2 Servings:

- Filet of fresh salmon, 3/4 lb
- 1 avocado, cubed

- 1 grapefruit, peeled, segmented
- 4 cups loosely packed mache (or any other spring greens)
- 1 lemon
- honey mustard vinaigrette
- Salt and pepper

Instructions:

1. Pre-heat oven to 350°F Place salmon on a parchment-lined baking sheet. Season the salmon with salt and pepper—Bake for 15 minutes, or until the mixture is opaque.
2. You can peel the grapefruit with a paring knife while the salmon bakes.
3. Layer greens, grapefruit wedges, and avocado on each plate. Dress lightly with vinaigrette. Serve the salmon in two pieces. Dress the salmon with lemon juice and place it on a plate.
4. Keep it in a sealed container and freeze for up to three months.

Nutritional Values Per Serving

Kcal	Fat	Cholesterol	Carbs
557	24 g	0 mg	33 g

Sugars	Fibers	Proteins	Sodium
7 g	9 g	52 g	775 mg

Preserving Salmon in Parchment

Preparation Time: 10 minutes

Cooking Time: 12 minutes

Ingredients For 4 Servings:

- 1 1/4 lb. salmon, cut into 4 pieces
- 1 small zucchini, thinly chopped
- 1 head Fennel, thinly cut, fronds reserved to garnish
- 2l emon, thinly chopped
- 1 tsp dried dill
- 4 tsp extra virgin oil
- 1 teaspoon salt
- 1/2 tsp freshly cracked black pepper
- parchment paper

Instructions:

1. Preheat the oven to 375°F

2. Divide the parchment into four large ovals measuring 15 by 10 inches. Fold in half.

3. Layer 1/4 of the zucchini, 1/4 of the fennel, and 1 piece of salmon on each parchment. Sprinkle 1/4 teaspoon salt, 1/4 cup pepper, 1/4 teaspoon of dill, and 1/4 teaspoon dill on the other half. Each salmon should be coated with 1 teaspoon olive and a few fennel leaves. Continue with the remaining three salmon fillets.

4. Fold the parchment in half and fold the top over the salmon. Then, roll the edges towards the center.

5. Place the pouches on baking sheets and bake for 15 minutes.

6. Use a fork to open the fennel fronds carefully and garnish with additional fennel fronds.

7. Freeze in freezer for up to 12 weeks.

Nutritional Values Per Serving

Kcal	Fat	Cholesterol	Carbs
331	17 g	0 mg	7 g

Sugars	Fibers	Proteins	Sodium
3 g	2 g	37 g	615 mg

Preserving Malabar Prawns

Preparation Time: 15 minutes

Cooking Time: 12 minutes

Ingredients For 4 Servings:

- 400 g raw king prawns
- 2 tsp turmeric
- 3-4 tsp Kashmiri chili powder
- 4 tsp lemon juice, plus a squeeze
- 40 g ginger, cut in half and grated
- 1 tbsp vegetable oils
- 4 curry leaves
- 2 to 4 green chilies, halved and deseeded
- 1 onion, finely chopped
- 1 tsp cracked pepper
- 40 g fresh coconut, grated
- 1/2 small bunch of coriander leaves, only

Instructions:

1. Rinse the prawns under cold water. Dry them with a towel. Mix the ginger, turmeric, chili powder, and lemon juice.

2. In a large saucepan, heat the oil, and then add the curry leaves and chili. After about 10 minutes, add the black pepper.

3. Stir-fry the prawns with any marinade until they are cooked. Add salt and pepper to taste. Sprinkle with coconut and coriander leaves.

4. Keep it in a sealed container and freeze for up to three months.

Nutritional Values Per Serving

Kcal	Fat	Saturated	Carbs
171	8 g	4 g	4 g

Sugars	Fibers	Proteins	Salt
3 g	3 g	19 g	0.8 g

Preserving Ginger, Sesame and Chili Prawn And Broccoli Stir-Fry

Preparation Time: 5 minutes

Cooking Time: 10 minutes

Ingredients For 2 Servings:

- 250 g Broccoli, thin-stemmed if desired, cut into even-sized pieces
- 2 balls of stem ginger, finely chopped, and 2 tbsp syrup
- 3 tbsp low-salt soy sauce
- 1 clove of garlic, crushed
- 1 red chili - thinly sliced. The rest deeded, finely chopped
- 2 tsp sesame seeds
- 1/2 tbsp sesame oils
- 200 g raw king prawns
- 100 g beansprouts
- To serve, cook rice or noodles

Instructions:

1. Bring a saucepan of water to a boil. Turn the broccoli into a saucepan and boil for 1 minute. It should retain its crunchiness. Mix the stem ginger, syrup, soy sauce, and garlic with the finely chopped chili.

2. Toast the sesame seeds in an oven-proof skillet or dry wok. Once they are nicely browned, heat the oil, add the prawns and cooked broccoli, and turn up the heat once they are nicely browned. Stir-fry the prawns for about a minute until they turn pink. Add the ginger sauce, and then add the beansprouts. Allow the beansprouts to cook for about 30 seconds or until they are cooked thoroughly. If necessary, you can add more ginger syrup or soy sauce. Sprinkle with the chopped chili, and serve with rice or noodles.

3. Portion it in a sealed container and freeze for up to two months.

Nutritional Values Per Serving

Kcal	Fat	Carbs	Sugars	Fibers	Proteins	Salt
274	9 g	20 g	16 g	5 g	26 g	2.6 g

Preserving Prawn, Coconut & Tomato Curry

Preparation Time: 10 minutes

Cooking Time: 20 minutes

Ingredients For 3 Servings:

- 2 tbsp vegetable oils
- 1 medium onion, thinly sliced
- 2 cloves of garlic, sliced
- 1 green chili, deseeded and sliced
- 3 Tbsp curry paste
- 1 tbsp tomato puree
- 200 ml vegetable stock
- 200 ml Coconut cream
- 350 g raw prawn
- Coriander sprigs and rice to serve

Instructions:

1. In a large skillet, heat the oil. Fry the garlic, onion, and half of the chili for 5 minutes or until tender. Cook for another minute. Add the tomato puree and stock to the coconut cream.

2. Allow the prawns to simmer on medium heat for 10 minutes, then add them. Cook the prawns for 3 minutes or until they become opaque. Serve with rice by adding green chilies and coriander sprigs.

3. Keep it in a sealed container and freeze for up to three months.

Nutritional Values Per Serving

Kcal	Fat	Carbs	Sugars	Fibers	Proteins	Salt
335	26 g	7 g	6 g	1 g	19 g	1.03 g

Preserving Prawn Noodles Soup

Preparation Time: 10 minutes

Cooking Time: 5 minutes

Ingredients For 1 Serving:

- 85 g thick rice noodles
- 500 ml Hot Chicken or Vegetable Stock
- 1 tsp fish sauce
- Juice 1/2 lime
- 1-star anise
- pinch sugar
- 1 handful of small raw prawns
- A handful of mint and coriander leaves
- Chopped red chili, to be served

Instructions:

1. Boil the noodles to al dente. Drain. In a saucepan, heat the stock and add the star anise, lime juice, salt, and pinch of sugar.
2. Bring to a boil, then add the noodles and the prawns.
3. Once the noodles are cooked, transfer them to a bowl. Top with the mint, coriander, and chili.
4. Keep it in a sealed container and freeze for up to three months.

Nutritional Values Per Serving

Kcal	Fat	Carbs	Sugars	Fibers	Proteins	Salt
256	3 g	30 g	3 g	2 g	31 g	3.33 g

Preserving Super-Quick Fish Curry

Preparation Time: 5 minutes

Cooking Time: 10 minutes

Ingredients For 4 Servings:

- 1 tbsp vegetable oils
- 1 large onion chopped
- 1 clove of garlic, chopped
- 1 - 2 tbsp Madras curry paste
- 400 g can tomato
- 200 ml vegetable stock
- Sustainable white fish fillets, skinned and cut into large chunks
- rice or naan bread

Instructions:

1. In a large skillet, heat the oil and fry the garlic and onion for 5 minutes until tender. Stir-fry the curry paste for about 1-2 minutes, then add the tomatoes and stock.

2. Bring to a simmer, and then add the fish. Allow the fish to cook gently for about 4-5 minutes or until it flakes easily. Serve immediately with rice, naan, or pasta.

3. Portion it in a sealed container and freeze for up to three months.

Nutritional Values Per Serving

Kcal	Fat	Carbs	Sugars	Fibers	Proteins	Salt
191	5 g	9 g	6 g	2 g	30 g	0.54 g

Preserving Grilled Mackerel In A Sweet Soy Glaze

Preparation Time: 10 minutes

Cooking Time: 15 minutes

Ingredients For 2 Servings:

- 4 mackerel fillets
- Juice 1 lime, and add extra wedges to taste
- 1 tbsp Extra-Virgin Olive Oil
- Butter, for greasing
- Steam baby bok Choi to Serve

For the sauce:

- 2 tbsp soy sauce
- 1 red chili - deseeded and cut into matchsticks
- Juice 1 lime
- Thumb-sized pieces of ginger, grated
- 2 tbsp muscovado sugar

Instructions:

1. The mackerel fillets should be scored a few times on the skin. Marinate the mackerel fillets for 5-10 minutes in the marinade.

2. Combine all the ingredients for the sauce in a small saucepan. Add a little water to bring it to a simmer. Allow the sauce to simmer for five minutes until it thickens slightly. Once it has cooled, please remove it from heat and allow it to cool.

3. Place the mackerel skin-side down on a baking tray. Grill the fillets for 5 minutes until they are opaque and cooked through.

4. Divide the bok choi among two plates. Place 2 mackerel fillets over them. Drizzle with the sauce. Serve with a wedged lime.

5. Keep it in a sealed container and freeze for up to six months.

Nutritional Values Per Serving

Kcal	Fat	Carbs	Sugars	Fibers	Proteins	Salt
474	30 g	22 g	22 g	0 g	29 g	3 g

Preserving Mediterranean Prawn Salad

Preparation Time: 15 minutes

Cooking Time: 10 minutes

Ingredients:

- Juice 1 lemon
- 4 tbsp Extra-Virgin Olive Oil
- pinch dried chili flakes
- 1 sliced red onions
- 1 sliced fennel bulbs

- 1 large rocket handful
- 200 g cooked prawn
- *Garlic bread to serve (optional)*

Instructions:

1. Combine lemon juice, olive oil, and dried chili flakes. Mix in red onion and fennel. Let it sit for about 7-8 minutes to soften.
2. Add rocket and prawns. Serve with garlic bread.
3. Keep it in a sealed container and freeze for up to three months.

Nutritional Values Per Serving

Kcal	Fat	Carbs	Sugars	Fibers	Proteins	Salt
311	24 g	8 g	6 g	5 g	18 g	1.6 g

Preserving Thai Fried Prawn & Pineapple Rice

Preparation Time: 10 minutes

Cooking Time: 15 minutes

Ingredients For 4 Servings:

- 2 tsp sunflower oil
- bunch spring onions , greens and whites separated, both sliced
- 1 green pepper , deseeded and chopped into small chunks
- 140 g pineapple , chopped into bite-sized chunks
- 3 tbsp Thai green curry paste
- 4 tsp light soy sauce , plus extra to serve
- 300 g cooked basmati rice (brown, white or a mix - about 140g uncooked rice)
- 2 large eggs , beaten
- 140 g frozen peas
- 225 g can bamboo shoots , drained
- 250 g frozen prawns , cooked or raw
- 2-3 limes , 1 juiced, the rest cut into wedges to serve
- *handful coriander leaves (optional)*

Instructions

1. Heat the oil in a wok or non-stick frying pan and fry the spring onion whites for 2 mins until softened. Stir in the pepper for 1 min, followed by the pineapple for 1 min more, then stir in the green curry paste and soy sauce.

2. Add the rice, stir-frying until piping hot, then push the rice to one side of the pan and scramble the eggs on the other side. Stir the peas, bamboo shoots and prawns into the rice and eggs, then heat through for 2 mins until the prawns are hot and the peas tender. Finally, stir in the spring onion greens, lime juice and coriander, if using. Spoon into bowls and serve with extra lime wedges and soy sauce.

3. Keep it in a sealed container and freeze for up to three months.

Nutritional Values Per Serving

Kcal	Fat	Carbs	Sugars	Fibers	Proteins	Salt
311	10 g	32 g	7 g	6 g	21 g	2.9 g

LEGUMES AND BEANS

Preserving White Bean Soup with Bacon

Preparation Time: 5 minutes

Cooking Time: 20 minutes

Ingredients For 4 Servings:

- Half lb. bacon cut into 1-inch strips
- 2 (14) oz. can white beans, cannellini, or Great Northern cans white beans, drained, rinsed
- 4 cups of chicken or vegetable stock
- 4 cloves garlic, thinly diced
- 1/2 teaspoon salt
- 1/2 topper
- *Parmesan rind (optional)*

Instructions:

1. The bacon should be cooked in a medium saucepan for 6-8 minutes. Set aside the bacon using a slotted spoon. Removing the bacon fat from the pot.

2. Bring to a boil chicken stock, bacon, beans, and garlic. Simmer for 15 minutes. You may need to salt the mixture if you don't have a parmesan cheese rind.

3. Serve with crusty bread or a simple salad. Enjoy!

4. Keep in the freezer and use within 8 weeks.

Nutritional Values Per Serving

Kcal	Fat	Carbs	Sugars
413	24 g	18 g	1 g

Fibers	Proteins	Sodium	Cholesterol
7 g	28 g	2405 g	62 mg

Preserving Garlic Spiced Pickled Beans

Preparation Time: 30 minutes

Cooking Time: 10 minutes

Ingredients For 7 Pints:

- Green beans weigh 4 to 5 lbs
- 6 cups of white vinegar
- 3 cups of water
- 3/4 cup granulated Sugar
- 14 cloves of garlic peeled and cut in half
- 1/8 teaspoon red bell pepper flakes per jar or to your liking
- *Pickling spice: 3 tablespoons*
- *Pickling salt: 1 tablespoon*

Instructions:

1. For processing, prepare 7-pint jars with lids and a canner.

2. Prepare green beans.

3. In 6-8 qt., combine vinegar, sugar, pickling spice, salt, and water. Bring to boil in a large pot. Reduce heat to low and simmer for 3 minutes.

4. Before packing the beans, add two garlic cloves (4 halves) to each jar. You can do one pot at a time. Pour the brine over, seal and then move on to the next.

5. Place the beans in the hot brine, leaving 1/2" of headspace. Use a spatula to remove air bubbles, wipe the jar rim and attach the lid. You should include a little of the pickling spices into each jar.

6. For 10 minutes, boiling water canner.

7. Transfer canner to towel-lined surface. Leave undisturbed for 24 hrs before sealing lids and labeling date. Use within one year to one-and-a-half year.

Nutritional Values Per Serving

Kcal	Fat	Carbs	Sugars	Fibers	Proteins	Salt
388	21 g	24 g	4 g	11 g	12 g	1.33 g

Preserving Easy Chickpea Coconut Milk Dhal

Preparation Time: 5 minutes

Cooking Time: 10 minutes

Ingredients For 3 Servings:

- Oil for cooking
- 3 cloves of garlic, chopped finely
- A small piece of ginger, peeled. Finely chopped
- Finely chopped 5 spring onions
- 10 cherry tomatoes, 5 chopped
- 1/2 bunch coriander leaves picked, stalks finely chopped
- Coconut milk cans up to 400 g
- Chickpeas – 400 g can drain and rinse
- 400 g can of cooked lentils. Drain and rinse.
- 2 tbsp curry powder
- 1 teaspoon ground turmeric
- 2 tsp ground cumin

- 1 lime, juiced
- A handful of spinach
- Wholemeal Pittas to Serve

Instructions:

1. Heat a little oil in a large pan or pot on medium heat. Reduce the heat to medium, add the ginger and garlic, and cook for about 3-5 minutes, stirring occasionally. Add the spring onions, cherry tomatoes, coriander leaves, stalks, and one teaspoon of salt. Continue cooking for 3 minutes more.

2. Stir in chickpeas, coconut milk, and lentils. Next, add the curry powder and turmeric. Bring to the boil. Reduce to a simmer, and let it cook for 5 minutes. Stir in the spinach, and let it wilt for about 5 minutes. Serve with pittas and season to taste.

3. Keep in freezing baggies and freeze for up to two months.

Nutritional Values Per Serving

Kcal	Fat	Carbs	Sugars	Fibers	Proteins	Salt
338	20 g	22 g	4 g	11 g	11 g	1.33 g

VEGETABLES AND FRUITS

Preserving Vegetable Biryani

Preparation Time: 20 minutes

Cooking Time: 15 minutes

Ingredients For 4 Servings:

- 250 g basmati rice
- Special mixed frozen vegetables of 400 g
- A generous amount of raisins
- 1 vegetable stock cube
- 2 tbsp Korma Curry Paste
- A generous amount of roasted salted cashew nuts

Instructions:

1. Boil the kettle. Take out a large microwaveable bowl, and add the rice, vegetables, and raisins.

2. Mix the rice mixture with 600ml/1 pint of boiling water. Add the stock cube and stir in the curry paste. To let the steam escape, cover the bowl with cling wrap. Cook the bowl on high power (850 watts) for 12 min. If your microwave is more powerful, you can add 2 minutes.

3. Remove the microwave from the stove and let the rice stand cover for five minutes to finish the cooking. Serve the rice with cashews, or let it cool in a freezer bag for two months.

Nutritional Values Per Serving

Kcal	Fat	Satured	Carbs
305	6 g	0 g	57 g

Sugars	Fibers	Proteins	Salt
0 g	2 g	9 g	1.42 g

Preserving Green Vegetable Soup

Preparation Time: 10 minutes

Cooking Time: 15 minutes

Ingredients For 6 Servings:

- 1 Bunch of Spring Onions, chopped
- 1 large potato, peeled and chopped
- 1 crushed garlic clove
- 1 l vegetable stock
- 250 g frozen peas
- 100 g fresh spinach
- 300 ml natural yogurt
- Few mint leaves, basil leaves, or cress to serve

Instructions:

1. Combine the spring onions and potato with the garlic in a large saucepan. Bring to a boil the vegetable stock.

2. Reduce heat to low and simmer for 15 minutes, covered. Or until the potato is soft enough to mash it with a spoon.

3. Bring the mixture back to a boil. Take out about 4 tbsp. Of the peas, and let excellent.

4. The yogurt and spinach should be mixed in a large bowl. Once the mixture is smooth, you can either use a stick blender or a blender to blend it. Season the mixture with black pepper.

5. Divide the mixture into two bowls. Add some of the cooked peas to each bowl. Finally, scatter your favorite soft herbs and cress over the top. If you prefer, serve with crusty bread or cool in the freezer for up to 5 months.

Nutritional Values Per Serving

Kcal	Fat	Satured	Carbs
127	3 g	1 g	16 g

Sugars	Fibers	Proteins	Salt
6 g	4 g	7 g	0.5 g

Easy Mango Preserve

Preparation Time: 5 minutes

Cooking Time: 15 minutes

Ingredients For 3 Servings:

- 3 large, ripe mangos. Peeled, seeded, and chopped.
- 1/4 cup granulated sugar
- 1 tablespoon lime or lemon juice

Instructions:

1. Combine all ingredients in a large saucepan. Bring to a boil on high heat. Mix well, reduce heat, and simmer the mixture for 10-15 minutes, stirring occasionally, or until slightly thickened.
2. Take preserves off the heat and let cool in a bowl or jar. Cover the container with plastic wrap or a lid once it has cooled completely.
3. You can enjoy it within 7-10 days.

Nutritional Values Per Serving

Kcal	Fat	Satured	Carbs	Sugars	Fibers	Proteins
56	0 g	0 g	14 g	9.7 g	0.2 g	0.1 g

Apple Preserve

Preparation Time: 15 minutes

Cooking Time: 30 minutes

Ingredients For 2 Servings:

- 500 g Modi apples, thinly diced
- 200 g brown sugar
- 200 g white sugar
- 1 Lemon juice
- 1/2-peeled lemon
- 1/2 vanilla bean
- 50 g raisins
- 4 tbs whisky

Instructions:

1. In a small bowl, combine the whisky and raisins.

2. Combine the apple dice with the sugars.

3. Mix all ingredients and let stand for 30 minutes.

4. Once the sugar has melted, place the saucepan on a heat source and add the raisins.

5. Let the stew simmer on medium heat for 30 minutes, occasionally stirring, until the sauce thickens and the apples become soft (approx. 30 minutes).

6. Once the stew has been cooked, remove the vanilla stick and pour the stew into sterilized glass containers. The caps should be fastened to the jars.

7. Place the jars upside-down on a wood board and let them cool.

8. Use stickers, stars, ribbons, and red ribbons to decorate the jars and keep for up to 1 year.

Nutritional Values Per Serving

Kcal	Fat	Satured	Carbs	Sugars	Fibers	Proteins
30	0 g	0 g	7 g	7 g	0 g	0 g

Preserving Dry Tomatoes In Olive Oil

Preparation Time: 45 minutes

Cooking Time: 5 minutes

Equipment:

- Food Dryer (or *optional oven method*)

Ingredients For 1 Serving:

- 3 to 5 pounds of paste/plum tomatoes (preferably), though larger tomatoes can be sliced and dried
- 1/4 cup or more red wine vinegar. You can also use apple cider vinegar or white wine vinegar
- 2 cups olive oils, or enough to cover tomatoes

Instructions:

1. Wash tomatoes and then cut off the top core.

2. Place the cut sides of the tomato halves on a tray for drying.

3. Dry at 135 degrees, according to the manufacturer. After drying for about four hours, flip the trays over and repeat the process. Except for a few small ones, most are dry by now. Allow drying for another 2 hours before you check again. You will see some dried tomatoes at this stage. I removed them and set them in a bowl. Then, dry the rest. The tomato halves that have been thoroughly dried should be firm and dry.

4. Use tongs to dip the tomato halves in the red wine vinegar. Let the vinegar sit for about a minute, then pour it into a clean quart jar. You can press the tomatoes down to fit more in the pot to remove any air.

5. When the jar is filled to the shoulders, drizzle olive oil over the tomatoes. To ensure safety, you should cover the tomatoes with olive oil before using them. You will use quite a lot of fat, but the oil can be used for cooking and salad dressings as soon as the tomatoes are gone.

6. Continue to dry tomatoes and dip them in oil. Cover with oil until you run out.

7. Keep jars cool and dark for up to one year. They are best kept within six months because they darken with age but are still safe to consume and delicious.

Nutritional Values Per Serving

Kcal	Fat	Satured	Carbs
160	3 g	1 g	15 g

Sugars	Fibers	Proteins	Salt
6 g	4 g	6 g	0.5 g

Quick & Easy Sliced Jalapenos

Preparation Time: 20 minutes

Cooking Time: 3 minutes

Ingredients For 7 Pints:

- 2 1/2 to 3 lb jalapenos
- 14 garlic cloves
- 4 cups cider vinegar
- 1/2 cup of water
- Pickling salt: 1 tablespoon

Instructions:

1. Wash jalapenos and cut off the stems. Then slice them into 1/4-inch rings. Each garlic clove should be cut in half.
2. Each of the 6 to 7-pint canning containers should be filled with chopped jalapenos, 4 clove halves (2 cloves per jar), and about 3/4 inch of headspace.

3. Heat the vinegar, water, and salt in a large saucepan until they boil. Then reduce the heat to a simmer and pour into jars.

4. You can pour the vinegar mixture using a spoon. If you are canning, leave 1/2 inch headspace. For refrigeration, cover the jalapenos entirely with the liquid.

5. Clean the rims and attach two-piece lids. Old lids can be reused if refrigerating, but water-bath canners should always use new covers.

6. For up to one year, label and refrigerate.

Nutritional Values Per Serving

Kcal	Fat	Satured	Carbs	Sugars
15	1 g	1 g	3 g	1 g

Fibers	Proteins	Sodium	Potassium
1 g	1 g	149 g	94 mg

Preserving Green Beans Without Blanching

Preparation Time: 15 minutes

Cooking Time: 7 minutes

Ingredients For 1-Quart Bag:

- Fresh green beans
- Freezer bags
- *straw, optional*

Instructions:

1. Green beans can be washed if necessary and dried thoroughly. Green beans can be cut in 1-1 inch lengths or any other size you prefer.
2. Place in zip-top freezer bags of quart size. Remove as much air as you can with a straw or other method. Seal the bag.
3. Place in freezer, label with the date and contents. Freeze for up to one year.
4. To use: You don't need to defrost. Freeze and bake in a 350-degree oven for 5-8 mins.

Nutritional Values Per Serving

Kcal	Fat	Satured	Carbs
127	3 g	1 g	16 g

Sugars	Fibers	Proteins	Salt
6 g	4 g	7 g	0.5 g

Preserving Snap Peas & Snow Peas Without Blanching

Preparation Time: 10 minutes

Cooking Time: 5 minutes

Equipment:

- Cutting Board
- Sharp Knife
- Large baking tray/cookie sheet
- freezer baggies/containers
- *straw, optional*

143

Ingredients For 4 Cups:

- 1 lb snap peas or snow peas

Instructions:

1. As usual, remove the tops and strings from the pods.
2. Dry them well and clean them if necessary. Don't clean them if you are unsure where or who they came from. If you wash them, dry them well by hand drying or air drying. (TIP: Using a salad spinner to dry faster will also help). The freezer will form ice crystals more quickly if filled with water.
3. Cut pods into 1- to 2-inch pieces. Although you could leave the pods whole, cutting them into smaller pieces helps to reduce the texture changes in the freezer.
4. Place in a freezer baggie. Label, remove air and freeze for up to 6 months.

Nutritional Values Per Serving

Kcal	Fat	Satured	Carbs
186	5 g	1 g	12 g

Sugars	Fibers	Proteins	Salt
6 g	4 g	8 g	0.5 g

Preserving Peppers, Hot & Sweet

Preparation Time: 10 minutes

Cooking Time: 2 minutes

Equipment:

- Cutting Board
- Sharp chef's knife
- Large baking pan
- Vacuum sealer, containers, and freezer bags
- straw (if using baggies)

Ingredients:

- 4-8 bell peppers or hot Peppers

Instructions:

1. Wash the peppers

2. Core, slice, chop or chop the peppers. Don't forget your gloves. Don't forget your gloves when working with hot peppers. Don't forget your gloves - even mild peppers can sting.

3. Place the peppers in an even layer on a cookie sheet, then place them in the freezer. Freeze until firm, approximately 12-24 hours.

4. Once the peppers have frozen, you can use a spatula or spoon to break them apart in jar or freezer containers. Place the peppers in the freezer and label them with the date and contents for up to six months.

Nutritional Values Per Serving

Kcal	Fat	Satured	Carbs
151	3 g	1 g	16 g

Sugars	Fibers	Proteins	Salt
6 g	4 g	5 g	0.5 g

Preserving Roast Beets

Preparation Time: 5 minutes

Cooking Time: 45 minutes

Ingredients For 4 Freezer Containers:

- 8 medium-large beets
- 1/4 cup of water

Instructions:

1. Clean the beets well and trim off the greens and roots, leaving about an inch at the tops. To ensure even cooking, chop any large beets in half.
2. Put the beets into a 13x9-inch baking dish. Add 1/4 cup water.
3. Bake in the oven at 400 degrees for 45 to 60 minutes, depending on how large the beets are. You can check whether they are done by inserting a small knife into the thickest

part of the beets. If you find smaller beets in the same pot as larger ones, take them out of the oven.

4. Take off the remaining tops and bottoms, then skin the beets with a small knife.

5. Slice the beets into small pieces or thin slices. Serve immediately or freeze.

6. You can freeze the beets for later use by placing them in a baggie or another freezer container. Remove as much air from the container as possible. Label the baggie and place it in the freezer. For best quality, use within 6-9 months.

Nutritional Values Per Serving

Kcal	Fat	Satured	Carbs
167	3 g	1 g	14 g

Sugars	Fibers	Proteins	Salt
6 g	5 g	4 g	0.5 g

Preserving Freeze Corn

Preparation Time: 30 minutes

Cooking Time: 10 minutes

Equipment:

- Cutting Board
- Chef's knife
- Freezer baggies

Ingredients For 1-Quart Bag:

- Depending on the size of your ears, you may need 2 to 3 corn cobs

Instructions:

1. Unblanched Whole Cobs are the easiest and fastest method.
2. Simply shuck the meat, place it in freezer bags, remove air, and put it in the freezer.

3. Uncooked Corn Kernels are the easiest, as you don't have first to cook the corn.

4. Bite the kernels from the cob and place them in a large bowl.

5. Spoon the kernels in freezer bags (or containers), remove any air, seal, and freeze.

6. Blanched Corn Kernels or Cooked Corn Kernels-This is the traditional method of freezing fresh corn.

7. Bring a large pot to boil water.

8. Cook the ears for 2-3 minutes in boiling water.

9. Rinse the mixture in a large bowl. Let them cool for a few minutes before you can handle them.

10. Cut the kernels from the cobs. Place in freezer bags, remove as much air (again, using a straw), seal, and freeze for 5- 8 months.

Nutritional Values Per Serving

Kcal	Fat	Satured	Carbs
200	3 g	1 g	18 g

Sugars	Fibers	Proteins	Salt
6 g	4 g	6 g	0.5 g

Preserving Garlic Dill Pickles

Preparation Time: 15 minutes

Cooking Time: 5 minutes

Ingredients For 1 Quart:

- Pickling cucumbers for 1 quart. Enough to fill a qt
- 4 cloves of garlic sliced in half
- Add 1 teaspoon to 2 large fresh dill heads. Dried dill seed can be added if you desire more dill flavor
- 1 1/4 cups cider vinegar
- 1/4 cup of water
- Pickling spices: 2 teaspoons
- 1 tablespoon + 1 teaspoon pickling salt
- 1/2 teaspoon sugar
- *Optional: 1/4 teaspoon red pepper flakes*

Instructions:

1. To sterilize pickles, prepare several quart containers equal to the number of spots.

2. Add the garlic, dill, and *optional red pepper flakes to the bottom of each jar.* Place the cucumbers on each jar, leaving 1/2 to 12 inches headspace.

3. Combine water, vinegar, spices, and salt in a large saucepan. Bring to a boil. Reduce heat and simmer for 5 minutes.

4. Place the brine in the jar, leaving 1/4 inch headspace. Add lids.

5. Allow to cool to room temperature. Label the lids with year and day, and store them in the fridge.

6. Pickles can be consumed within 3-4 weeks. They will continue to improve with storage for several months.

Nutritional Values Per Serving

Kcal	Fat	Satured	Carbs
105	3 g	1 g	17 g

Sugars	Fibers	Proteins	Salt
6 g	4 g	10 g	0.5 g

Preserving Chilies & Tomatoes

Preparation Time: 1 hour

Cooking Time: 1 hour

Ingredients For 7 Pints:

- 12 cups peeled, cored, and quartered tomatoes, approximately 32 medium-sized tomatoes
- 1 cup finely chopped chili bell peppers anaheim or ancho
- 1 tablespoon of canning salt
- 1 teaspoon black pepper
- 1 teaspoon dried oregano
- 1 teaspoon coriander
- Add 1/4 teaspoon of Citric Acid to each pint, 1/2 teaspoon for quarts, or 1 tablespoon bottled Lemon Juice for pints (2 Tablespoons for quarts)

Instructions:

1. Peel, wash, and quarter the tomatoes. Combine in a large stockpot.

2. Wash, stem, and seed chilies. If desired, you can leave the seeds in place to increase the spiciness. You can either chop the chilies by hand or chop them into large pieces that you can use in a food processor.

3. Chilies, salt, pepper, oregano, and coriander should be added to the tomatoes in a stockpot. Bring to a boil, then reduce heat to simmer for 10 minutes.

4. While the tomato mixture simmers, prepare lids, canners, and jars.

5. Clean, hot pint canning containers with 1/4 teaspoon Citric Acid or 1 tablespoon of lemon juice. Add 1/2 teaspoon citric acid or two tablespoons of lemon juice using quart jars.

6. Place the tomato-chili mix in each jar. Leave 1/2 inch headspace. Use a spatula to remove any bubbles and wipe the rims. Attach lids.

7. Cover jars in the canner and bring to boil. Let cool for 40 minutes (50 for quarts) before adjusting the heat to keep it at a gentle boil. Turn off the heat, take off the lid and let the jars sit in the canner for 5 minutes.

8. Transfer jars to a towel-lined counter. Let cool for 12 to 24 hours. Take out rings and verify that the lids are sealed. Gently pull the covers up with your fingers. Any that did not seal should be refrigerated.

9. You can label and date the containers and freeze them for one year.

Nutritional Values Per Serving

Kcal	Fat	Carbs	Sugars	Fibers	Proteins	Sodium
7	0.1 g	1.6 g	1 g	0.5 g	0.3 g	82 g

Preserving Lemon Garlic Roasted Vegetables and Delicious Soup

Preparation Time: 30 minutes

Cooking Time: 30 minutes

Ingredients For 4 Portions:

- Roasted Vegetables: 3 medium zucchini and summer squash
- 2 sweet bell peppers in orange, red, or Jaune
- 2 carrots
- 1 onion
- 4 cloves of garlic
- 1/3 c Mixed fresh herbs, such as basil, rosemary, and thyme
- 1 lemon's zest and juice
- 3 tablespoons olive oils
- 1/2 teaspoon salt
- 1/2 teaspoon black pepper

For the soup:

- 3 cups Lemon Garlic Roasted Vegetables
- For vegetarians, 4 cups of vegetable broth or chicken broth
- Salt and pepper to your liking
- *Optional: 1 Cup Peeled and Diced Potato and 1 Cup of Milk*

Instructions:

To roast the vegetables:

1. Preheat the oven to 425°F.
2. All the vegetables should be chopped into similar shapes and placed in a large roasting tray.
3. Mix the olive oil, herbs, lemon zest, juice, salt, pepper, and stir.
4. Roast vegetables for between 30-40 minutes, or until they are very tender.
5. Allow to cool, then place in quart-sized freezer containers of baggies in 3-cup portions: label and freeze for up to six months. There should be enough to fill 2 containers/baggies.

To make the soup:

1. Bring the broth, vegetables, and potato to a boil in a large saucepan. Reduce heat and cover the pot. Let it simmer for 10 minutes (or 15 if you use potatoes).
2. Blend in an immersion blender or allow to cool in the pot.
3. Salt and pepper to your liking. If you like, add milk.

Nutritional Values Per Serving

Kcal	Fat	Satured	Carbs
89	3 g	1 g	11 g

Sugars	Fibers	Proteins	Salt
6 g	4 g	7 g	0.5 g

Preserving Roasted Red Peppers in Wine

Preparation Time: 45 minutes

Cooking Time: 15 minutes

Ingredients For 4 Half-Pint Jars:

- 2 lb sweet red, yellow, or orange bell peppers (about 8)
- 1 large minced clove of garlic
- 1 1/2 cups dry white wine
- 1 cup cider vinegar

- 1 cup finely chopped onion
- 1 Tablespoon of Sugar
- 1 teaspoon of canning salt
- 1/2 teaspoon dried basil or an Italian herb blend

Instructions:

1. Peel, wash, and cut the peppers in half. Large peppers might need to be halved for flat rest. Broil the peppers skin-side up in a single layer.
2. Add the blackened peppers to a large baggie or tightly sealed container. Let the skins cool for at least 15 minutes.
3. Prepare four half-pint canner jars. Slice the garlic and onion.
4. Transfer the peppers to a cutting board. Peel the skins and cut them into strips. Place the strips in a bowl.
5. Mix all ingredients in a large saucepan. Bring to a boil on high heat. Reduce heat to low and simmer gently for five minutes.
6. Place the peppers in a single jar, one at a time, within 1 to 3 inches of the top.
7. The boiling brine should be poured over the peppers leaving a 1/2 inch headspace. Use a non-metallic spatula to move the jar around to remove any air bubbles. Be careful not to compress the peppers. You can add more brine if necessary.
8. Clean the rim and attach the lid and ring. Place on canner rack. Continue with the remaining jars. Lower rack into canner. Bring to a boil on high heat. Boil for 15 minutes at a gentle boil. Adjust heat as necessary. Turn off the heat and remove the lid. Let the jars cool in the canner for five minutes. Then transfer the pots onto a towel-lined surface.
9. Keep in the refrigerator for 24 hours. Check lids for seal and place in a cool, dry place. Use within one year to 18 months.

Nutritional Values Per Serving

Kcal	Fat	Satured	Carbs
78	3 g	1 g	15 g

Sugars	Fibers	Proteins	Salt
6 g	4 g	8 g	0.5 g

Preserving Tomatoes & Chilies

Preparation Time: 1 hour

Cooking Time: 1 hour

Ingredients For 7 Pints:

- 12 cups peeled, cored, and quartered tomatoes, approximately 32 medium-sized tomatoes
- 1 cup finely chopped chili peppers anaheim or ancho
- 1 tablespoon of canning salt
- 1 teaspoon black pepper

- 1 teaspoon dried oregano
- 1/2 teaspoon coriander
- To add citric acid to jars, 1/4 teaspoon per pint 1/2 teaspoon for the quarts OR 1 teaspoon bottled lemon juice to pints (2 Tablespoons for the quarts)

Instructions:

1. Peel, wash, and quarter the tomatoes. Combine in a large stockpot.
2. Wash, stem, and seed chilies. Chop finely by hand, chop into large pieces and then process in a food processor.
3. Chilies, salt, pepper, oregano, and coriander should be added to the tomatoes in a stockpot. Bring to a boil, then reduce heat to simmer for 10 minutes.
4. Let cool slightly on the heat before you transfer to freezer-safe containers. If using plastic, let it cool completely before you transfer.
5. You can label and date the containers and freeze them for one year.

Nutritional Values Per Serving

Kcal	Fat	Carbs	Sugars	Fibers	Proteins	Sodium
7	0.1 g	1.6 g	1 g	0.5 g	0.3 g	82 mg

Preserving Fresh Berries and Zabaglione

Preparation Time: 15 minutes

Cooking Time: 20 minutes

Ingredients For 8 Servings:

- 5 egg yolks
- 1/3 cup granulated Sugar
- 1/3 cup Marsala wine (dry, sweet)
- 1 cup heavy cream (whipping cream), whipped until stiff
- 5 1/4 cups fresh strawberries (blackberries and blueberries, quartered strawberries, and raspberries)

Instructions:

1. Place a double boiler, or a medium-sized stainless-steel dish, over a pot simmering with water. The eggs will scramble if the bottom of your bowl touches the water.

2. Use a handheld electric mixer or a thin wire whip to beat the egg yolks together for approximately three minutes or until they are pale yellow. Slowly add the Marsala wine. Set the bowl over barely simmering water (Remember: water shouldn't touch the bottom of the bowl).

3. Keep beating for approximately 10 to 15 mins until eggs triple in volume and thicken to 140°F. This temperature can be checked with an instant thermometer. They will initially become frothy and then, as they cook, will stiffen slightly but retain the air. You might endanger the eggs by stopping whipping the egg or boiling the water. Make sure you whip the eggs around in the bowl with the beater. *NOTE: If eggs curdle, remove the insert from the boiling water for a few seconds.* Continue whisking.

4. The mixture should be taken off the heat and cooled completely in the fridge. Use a rubber spatula to fold the prepared whipped cream into the mixture gently.

5. Keep it in a sealed container and freeze for up to three months.

6. *NOTE: You can make zabaglione ahead of time and keep it covered in the refrigerator for several hours. Before serving, let the sauce cool to room temperature.*

Nutritional Values Per Serving

Kcal	Fat	Satured	Carbs
30	3 g	1 g	2 g

Sugars	Fibers	Proteins	Salt
1 g	4 g	1 g	0.5 g

Preserving Sausage, Kale, and Potato Skillet

Preparation Time: 10 minutes

Cooking Time: 20 minutes

Ingredients For 6 Servings:

- 3 tbsp olive oils
- 24 oz. Potatoes cut in half, boiled in salted boiling water until tender
- Salt & pepper to your liking
- 2 tsp dried thyme
- 6 chicken sausage links, 1" sliced
- 1onion, medium, thinly cut
- 1 tsp garlic, minced
- 1 bunch curly Kale, with the ribs, removed
- *Optional 1 lemon*

Instructions:

1. In a large 15-inch pan, heat 2 tablespoons of olive oil on medium heat. Cook potatoes cut side down on medium heat until golden brown. Continue to cook until all sides are crisp, approximately 5-7 minutes. Depending on how large your pan is, you may need to cook this in several batches—season potatoes with salt and pepper.

2. Add another tablespoon of olive oil and the chicken sausage to the potatoes. For about 4-5 minutes, cook the sausage until crispy on all sides. After the brittle link, add the onions to the pan and cook for about 5 minutes, stirring frequently.

3. Reduce heat to medium. Add the garlic and stir until fragrant. Add the kale. Stir frequently and cook until the kale becomes wilted (about 3 minutes).

4. Serve the dish by squeezing a lemon on top.

5. If you find that the kale is too dense, take out the potato sausage mixture. Then saute the kale in its oil before adding it to the skillet.

6. Portion it in a sealed container and freeze for up to three months.

Nutritional Values Per Serving

Kcal	Fat	Cholesterol	Carbs
212	10 g	18 g	26 g

Sugars	Fibers	Proteins	Sodium
2 g	4 g	8 g	139 mg

Preserving Lemons

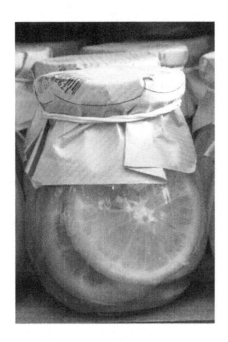

Preparation Time: 15 minutes

Cooking Time: 1 hour

Ingredients For Servings 1 Pint:

- Organic: 3 small lemons

- 1/3 cup freshly squeezed lemon juice (about 3 lemons)

- 1/4 cup coarse salt (sea salt, kosher salt, or pickling salt)

Instructions:

1. A wide-mouth, one-pint canning jar with a screw lid or airlock lid (with a wide mouth) in hot soapy water. Rinse with hot water. Turn the pot upside-down on a towel.

NOTE: Any size container can be used - you need to adjust the number of lemons, salt, and lemon juice.

2. Use a vegetable brush to scrub the lemons. Rinse well with warm water and dry using a clean cloth. Slice the lemons in half lengthwise and cut them into quarters. Could you place them in a large bowl? Toss the lemon quarters in salt with a spatula.

3. Use your hands or tongs to place the quarters of lemon into the jar. This will allow for the full release of their juices. Salt the lemons with a bit of salt, and then place the rest of the lemons in the jar. Use the spatula to transfer the remaining salt from the bowl into a pot.

4. To completely cover the lemons, pour just enough freshly squeezed lemon juice into a jar. Use a damp cloth to clean the rim. Seal the lid tightly.

5. The jar should be kept in a dark, cool place for 3 weeks. If necessary, you can leave it there longer. Every 3-4 days, flip the jar upside down (on end), and let it sit for a while before turning the jar upside down. When the rinds of the lemons have softened and separated from the flesh and pith, the fruit is ready to be used.

6. Use the preserved lemons by removing a quarter of lemon from the jar as necessary. To avoid bacteria contamination, use tongs to remove the lemon quarter from the pot. The lemon quarter should be rinsed under cool water to remove pulp or seeds. Only use the pickled lemon skin. The lemon pulp is fine, but it's best to use the pickled lemons sparingly. They can be very refreshing.

7. Once the jar is opened, keep the preserved lemons in the refrigerator for one year.

Kcal	Fat	Satured	Carbs
70	3 g	1 g	4 g

Sugars	Fibers	Proteins	Salt
1 g	4 g	1 g	0.5 g

Preserving Pickled Armenian Cucumbers With Fresh Dill

Preparation Time: 15 minutes

Cooking Time: 5 minutes

Ingredients For 1 Jar:

- 2 young Armenian cucumbers, approximately 8 inches in length, unpeeled and with the ends trimmed
- 1 cup white vinegar

- 1 cup of water
- 1 cup sugar, granulated
- 20 whole tricolor peppercorns
- 2 fresh sprigs of dill weed

Instructions:

1. Clean cucumbers and then use a mandolin to slice them thinly. Set aside in a large bowl.
2. Combine vinegar, water, and sugar in a medium saucepan. Stir over medium heat until sugar dissolves. Set aside to cool off from the heat.
3. Mix the mixture with the cukes and let cool. Cover the bowl with the dill springs.
4. Put in the refrigerator for three hours before serving.
5. Keep it in a sealed container and freeze for up to six months.

Nutritional Values Per Serving

Kcal	Fat	Satured	Carbs
67	3 g	1 g	3 g

Sugars	Fibers	Proteins	Salt
2 g	4 g	0.7 g	0.5 g

Preserving Sweet Pickled Banana Chile Peppers

Preparation Time: 30 minutes

Cooking Time: 10 minutes

Ingredients For 2 (1/2 pints) Jars:

- 1/2 pound of banana chile peppers
- 2 cups white distilled vinegar
- 1/3 cup sugar, granulated
- 12 teaspoon celery seeds
- 1 teaspoon of yellow mustard seed

Instructions:

1. Clean the banana chile peppers by washing them well. Remove the stem end and cut crossways into 1/4-inch rings (approximately 2 cups, depending on how big your peppers are).

2. To test how whole you like the peppers, put them in a couple of jars. It is possible to adjust the pickling liquid and the peppers. It all depends on how large the peppers are. You can use pint-jars, so I doubled the pickling juice and used 4 cups of peppers.

3. Use hot soapy water to sterilize 2 (1/2 pints) largemouth jars. Rinse well, then pour boiling water into them. Let's sit until you are ready to use it.

4. Add the vinegar, sugar, and celery seeds to a large saucepan. Bring to a boil.

5. Drain the water from the jars while you wait. Place the peppers in the jars tightly.

6. Put the hot pickling juice in the jars and the peppers.

7. Use a damp towel to clean the edges of the jars—screw on the bands and place lids. Let jars cool on the counter. When sealed, jar lids will vibrate and feel hollow in the middle. Check that the jars are sealed properly. If the pots do not close properly, place them in the refrigerator. It will pickle for two weeks.

8. Place in a dark, cool place for at most two weeks before opening. You can use it within two months.

Nutritional Values Per Serving

Kcal	Fat	Satured	Carbs
71	3 g	1 g	7 g

Sugars	Fibers	Proteins	Salt
2 g	4 g	3 g	0.5 g

Preserving Instant Frozen Strawberry Yogurt

Preparation Time: 2 minutes

Ingredients For 4 Servings:

- 250g frozen mixed berry
- 250g 0%-fat Greek yogurt
- 1 tbsp honey/agave syrup

Instructions:

1. Blend the yogurt, berries, and honey in a food processor until smooth texture. Serve in bowls.
2. Keep it in a sealed container and freeze for up to two months.

Kcal	Fat	Carbs	Sugars	Fibers	Proteins	Salt
70	0 g	10 g	10 g	2 g	7 g	0.1 g

Preserving Couscous Salad

Preparation Time: 10 minutes

Cooking Time: 10 minutes

Ingredients:

- 100 g couscous
- 200 ml hot, low-salt vegetable stock (from a cube)
- 2 spring onions
- 1 red pepper
- 1/2 cucumber
- 50 g feta cheese, cubed
- 2 tbsp pesto
- 2 tbsp pine nuts

Instructions:

1. Place the couscous in a bowl. Add the stock to cover it. Cover and let sit for 10 minutes until the couscous is fluffy.
2. Slice the onion and pepper and chop the cucumber. These can be added to the couscous.
3. Next, stir in the pesto and crumble in the Feta. Finally, sprinkle the pine nuts on top.
4. Portion it in a sealed container and freeze for up to four weeks.

Nutritional Values Per Serving

Kcal	Fat	Carbs	Sugars	Fibers	Proteins	Salt
327	17 g	33 g	7 g	2 g	13 g	0.88 g

Home Preserved Quick Tomato Risotto

Preparation Time: 5 minutes

Cooking Time: 20 minutes

Ingredients For 4 Servings:

- 250 g risotto rice
- 1 onion, finely chopped
- 50 g butter
- 250 ml vegetable stock
- 500 ml carton passata
- 500 g cherry tomato punnet
- 100 g ball mozzarella, drain, and cut into large pieces
- To serve, add grated parmesan or a vegetarian substitute and shredded basil

Instructions:

1. Place the rice, half of the butter, and the onion in a microwave-safe large bowl—Cook in the microwave at High for 3 minutes. Add the stock and passata to the bowl. Continue cooking covered for 10 minutes. Mix in the mozzarella and tomatoes. Stir it. For 8 minutes, microwave on High until rice is tender and tomatoes are softened.
2. Allow the risotto mixture to rest, then add the butter, basil, and parmesan. Season to taste, then serve directly from the bowl.
3. Keep it in a sealed container and freeze for up to six weeks.

Nutritional Values Per Serving

Kcal	Fat	Carbs	Sugars	Fibers	Proteins	Salt
435	17 g	62 g	10 g	3 g	13 g	1.34 g

Pasta Salad With Tuna, Capers and Balsamic Vinegar

Preparation Time: 10 minutes

Cooking Time: 10 minutes

Ingredients For 4 Servings:

- 350 g orecchiette pasta
- MSC-approved tuna in spring water, 225 g jar
- 1 tbsp caper, drained
- 15 peppadew Peppers in a Jar, Chopped
- 1 celery heart, sliced
- 140 g yellow, red, or a combination of cherry tomato, halved
- 75 ml balsamic Vinegar
- 3 Tbsp Extra-Virgin Olive Oil
- 100 g bag rocket leaves
- Good handful of basil leaves

Instructions:

1. Follow the package instructions to cook the pasta. Drain and rinse under cold water.

2. Transfer the pasta to a large bowl after draining.

3. Mix the rest of the ingredients, except for the basil. Toss together. Sprinkle with basil, and serve.

4. Keep it in a sealed container and freeze for up to three weeks.

Nutritional Values Per Serving

Kcal	Fat	Carbs	Sugars	Fibers	Proteins	Salt
527	10 g	82 g	16 g	3 g	24 g	0.6 g

Home Preserved Veg & Soft Cheese Frittata

Preparation Time: 10 minutes

Cooking Time: 20 minutes

Ingredients For 4 Servings:

- 100 g chopped streaky bacon or lardon
- 1 tbsp olive oil
- 2 large courgettes, cut into chunks
- 350 g frozen sweetcorn
- 400 g frozen spinach, defrosted and drained
- 8 eggs
- 150 g soft cheese pack with garlic and herbs

Instructions:

1. Fry the bacon or lardons until golden brown in a large nonstick frying pan. Add the courgettes and cook for about a minute until they become soft—Season the sweetcorn and spinach with salt, and heat through.
2. Turn the grill on medium heat. Mix the eggs and then add the vegetables. Sprinkle the cheese over and cook for about 5 minutes, or until the egg is just set around the edges. Place the frittata on a grill and cook for 5 minutes. Slice the frittata into wedges, and serve with a simple green vegetable salad.
3. Keep it in a sealed container and freeze for up to fiveweeks.

Nutritional Values Per Serving

Kcal	Fat	Carbs	Sugars	Fibers	Proteins	Salt
540	40 g	18 g	5 g	4 g	29 g	1.62 g

Home Preserved Frozen Blackberry Fool

Preparation Time: 10 minutes

Ingredients For 6 Servings:

- 300 g blackberry
- Juice 1 lemon
- 85 g golden caster sugar
- 300 ml double cream
- Shortbread biscuits to serve

Instructions:

1. Mix the blackberries and lemon juice with half of the sugar. The rest of the sugar is added to the cream. Mix the whipped cream with the blackberry mixture to create a mauve cream—place in a container and freeze.

2. Serve the whipped cream and blackberry mixture in small glasses with the shortbread and the remaining blackberries.

3. Portion it in a sealed container and freeze for up to three months.

Nutritional Values Per Serving

Kcal	Fat	Carbs	Sugars	Fibers	Proteins	Salt
475	40 g	26 g	26 g	3 g	2 g	0 g

Preserving Peach and Raspberry Fruit Salad with Mascarpone

Preparation Time: 10 minutes

Ingredients For 4 Servings:

- 2 ripe nectarines or peaches
- 50 g caster Sugar
- 1 tsp lemon-thyme leaves
- 100 g Mascarpone

- 100 ml double cream

- drop vanilla extract

- 16 raspberries, halved

- A small handful of pistachios, roughly chopped

- 1 tbsp maple syrup

Instructions:

1. The nectarines or peaches can be sliced and arranged on four plates. Sprinkle some sugar on top and scatter most of the thyme leaves.

2. In a bowl, whisk together the cream, vanilla extract, and remaining sugar until light and fluffy. Pipe or spoon blobs of the mixture onto the nectarines or peaches, and then arrange the raspberries on the plates. Serve with some pistachios and the rest of the thyme leaves.

3. Keep it in a sealed container and freeze for up to two weeks.

Nutritional Values Per Serving

Kcal	Fat	Carbs	Sugars	Fibers	Proteins	Salt
337	26 g	21 g	20 g	2 g	3 g	0.1 g

Mushroom & Sausage Pasta

Preparation Time: 10 minutes

Cooking Time: 20 minutes

Ingredients For 4 Servings:

- 4 sausages with skin removed and meat squeezed out
- 4 bacon rashers, diced
- 200 g mushrooms, chopped
- 350 g pasta shapes
- 50 g grated parmesan plus additional shavings to be served
- 2 egg yolks
- Small bunch of parsley, finely chopped
- 2 tbsp half-fat creme fraiche

Instructions:

1. Dry fry the sausage meat in non-stick oil for 8-10 minutes until browned. Use a wooden spoon to break it up and then set it aside. Sauté bacon and mushrooms until golden. Return the sausage meat to the pan and heat up.

2. Follow the package instructions to cook the pasta. Mix the Parmesan cheese, egg yolks, most parsley, and creme fraiche to make the sauce. Drain the pasta once it is cooked.

3. Mix the meat and pasta over low heat. Add the sauce. Add the sauce to the pasta and mix quickly. If it becomes too thick, add a bit more cooking water. Serve in bowls with extra Parmesan shavings, remaining parsley, and the rest of the Parsley.

4. Portion it in a sealed container and freeze for up to two weeks.

Nutritional Values Per Serving

Kcal	Fat	Carbs	Sugars	Fibers	Proteins	Salt
641	29 g	72 g	4 g	4 g	28 g	1.96 g

Preserving Pumpkin Curd

Preparation Time: 10 minutes

Cooking Time: 20 minutes

Ingredients For 3 Cups:

- 2 lbs fresh pumpkin, halved and seeded. Cut into 1 1/2 inch pieces. 2 cups canned pumpkin puree
- 2 inches of fresh ginger root, peeled and grated
- Juice of 1 lime (grated zest)
- 2 cups granulated sugar
- 1/8 teaspoon nutmeg, mixed
- 1/4 cup (1 1/2 sticks, or cubes), unsalted butter cut into cubes
- 4 eggs, beaten

Instructions:

1. Place the cut pumpkin pieces in a saucepan using fresh pumpkin. Bring to a boil 1 cup of water. Reduce heat to low, and simmer until the pumpkin is tender. Drain the liquid and remove it from the heat.

2. Blend the pumpkin solids with a blender. Add just enough of the reserved pumpkin liquid so that the blades can run smoothly. These steps can be skipped if you are using canned pumpkin puree.

3. Use a garlic press to squeeze the ginger. The ginger solids should be thrown out.

4. Place the lime zest, juice, ginger juice, and pumpkin puree in a medium saucepan on medium heat. Add the sugar. Stir the sugar until it dissolves completely. Then, remove the mixture from the heat. Stir in butter until it is melted.

5. Use a fine strainer to pour the egg whites through the filter and into the bowl with the pumpkin mixture. Cook the mixture for approximately 30 minutes, frequently stirring at the beginning and then continue at the end. It should not boil, or it will curdle.

6. Turn off the heat and place the Pumpkin Curd mixture in sterilized glass containers. Let cool. As it cools, the pumpkin curd will thicken.

7. Use immediately, or keep in the fridge for up to one week.

Nutritional Values Per Serving

Kcal	Fat	Carbs	Sugars	Fibers	Proteins	Salt
337	26 g	21 g	20 g	2 g	3 g	0.1 g

SALSAS AND SAUCES

Preserving Plain Roasted Tomato Sauce

Preparation Time: 30 minutes

Cooking Time: 45 minutes

Ingredients For 2 Quarts:

- 1 tablespoon olive oil
- Fresh tomatoes weighing 4 to 5 pounds
- *Salt (optional): 1 to 2 teaspoons*

Instructions:

1. Heat to 425° F.
2. Prepare as many baking pans as you need to make your tomato sauce. If your oven is large enough, place 1 tablespoon of olive oil at the bottom of each one.

3. Large tomatoes can be cut in half. Core the tomatoes and remove blossom ends. Place cut sides down in oil-based pans. To make more petite tomatoes, slice the tops and core them. Then, place the sliced tops in a pan.

4. Place a single layer on top of the tomatoes in each pan. You can touch them, but do not stack them.

5. If desired, sprinkle with a teaspoon or so of salt.

6. Bake for 40 to 45 minutes. Turn halfway through (in non-convection ovens) and rotate if you use more than one pan. Continue roasting until the tomatoes' tops start to blister and puff up.

7. Allow cooling in the oven for 10 minutes. Tongs can be used to scrape the skins of blackened tomatoes while they are cooling.

8. Place equal amounts of tomatoes and juices in a blender/food processor. Process until smooth. Transfer to containers or freezer jars, leaving at least 1-inch for expansion.

9. Add lids and label with date and name (masking tape, a sharpie), and freeze.

10. The sauce can be stored in the freezer for up to a year.

Nutritional Values Per Serving

Kcal	Fat	Carbs	Sugars	Fibers	Proteins	Salt
70	0 g	10 g	10 g	2 g	7 g	0.1 g

Preserving Tomato Bruschetta Topping

Preparation Time: 45 minutes

Cooking Time: 30 minutes

Ingredients For 9 Half-Pints:

- 8 cups chopped, cored, and peeled tomato/paste
- 5 cloves minced garlic
- 1 cup dry white wine as an alternative
- 1 cup cider vinegar
- 1/2 cup of water
- 2 tablespoons sugar
- 2 tablespoons balsamic Vinegar
- 1 tablespoon dried basil
- 1 tablespoon dried oregano

Instructions:

1. Prepare tomatoes.

2. Prepare lids, jars, and canner.

3. Combine all ingredients in a large stainless pot, except tomatoes. Over high heat, bring to a boil, stirring frequently.

4. Cover the saucepan and reduce heat. Boil gently for five minutes. Fill the jars with water and keep them warm at the lowest heat.

5. Place tomatoes in hot jars. Leave a 1/2 inch headspace. Pour the hot vinegar mixture into the jars. Make sure you leave 1/2-inch headspace. Use a non-metallic spatula to remove air bubbles and add any liquid needed to maintain the 1/2-inch headspace. Attach lids to jars and wipe rims.

6. Bring to boil and let stand for 20 minutes. Turn off the heat and let cool for 5 minutes.

7. After 24 hours, check seals and store them in a cool, dry place for up to 5 months.

Nutritional Values Per Serving

Kcal	Fat	Carbs	Sugars	Fibers	Proteins	Salt
89	0 g	9 g	6 g	2 g	5 g	0.1 g

Preserving Frugal Homemade Pesto

Preparation Time: 30 minutes

Ingredients For 1 1/4 Cups:

- 6 cloves of garlic peeled
- 1/4 cup sunflower seeds
- 1/2 cup grated Parmesan cheese
- 1 teaspoon salt, or to your taste
- 1 1/2 cups of packed basil leaves, washed and dried
- 1 tablespoon lemon juice to freeze pesto after opening
- 3/4 to 1 cup olive oil plus additional if frozen

Instructions:

1. Blend garlic until finely chopped in a food processor. Add the seeds, cheese, salt, and process until smooth. Then pulse a few times to chop. Next, add the basil. If desired, add lemon juice.

2. While the machine is running, add oil in a fine stream. Blend until pesto is smooth. Salt can be adjusted to taste if necessary (less if you use salted sunflower seeds).

3. You can freeze pesto by placing about 1/2 cup in freezer-safe containers. Add a thin layer of olive oil to the tops. Attach lids and label the container with the date. Pesto frozen can be kept for up to a year.

Nutritional Values Per Serving

Kcal	Fat	Carbs	Sugars	Fibers	Proteins	Salt
70	0 g	10 g	10 g	2 g	7 g	0.1 g

Preserving Vodka Sauce

Preparation Time: 20 minutes

Cooking Time: 1 hour

Ingredients for 10 Servings:

- ½ cup butter
- 1 onion, diced
- 1 cup vodka
- 2 (28 ounce) cans crushed tomatoes
- 1 pint heavy cream

Instructions:

1. In a skillet over medium heat, saute onion in butter until slightly brown and soft. Pour in vodka and let cook for 10 minutes. Mix in crushed tomatoes and cook for 30 minutes. Pour in heavy cream and cook for another 30 minutes.
2. Put the sauce in a container, cover it with lids and label it with the date and name, can be kept for up to a year.

Nutritional Values Per Serving

Kcal	Fat	Carbs	Cholesterol	Proteins	Sodium
355	27.3 g	13.9 g	89.6 g	3.8 g	291 mg

Preserving Pizza Sauce From Fresh or Frozen Tomatoes

Preparation Time: 1 hour

Cooking Time: 1 hour and 15 mins

Ingredients For 8 Pints Or 16 Half-Pints:

- 22 lb tomatoes whole or fresh
- 3 cups chopped onion
- 6 cloves minced garlic
- 1/4 cup olive oil
- 2 tablespoons dried basil
- 1 tablespoon of dried oregano
- 1 tablespoon dried thyme
- 1/2-1 tablespoon black pepper
- 1 tablespoon honey or sugar, or to your taste
- 2 tablespoons salt
- 1 to 2 teaspoons of crushed red pepper flakes

- Bottled lemon Juice or Citric Acid: 1/4 teaspoon citric acid for each pint and 12-oz Jars; 1/2 teaspoon lemon juice OR 1/8 teaspoon of Citric Acid for each half-pint Jars

Instructions:

1. To make tomato puree using frozen tomatoes: If they have been cleaned and cored before freezing, let them thaw for 24 hours. Drain any juices, and then strain the mixture through a strainer to remove all seeds and skins.

2. Make tomato puree using fresh tomatoes. Wash, core, and halve tomatoes. Heat to boiling. You can use a 12-quart stockpot for 22 pounds and a 6-quart soup pan for 22 pounds. Strain through a strainer to remove any seeds or peels.

3. Heat olive oil in a large 12-quart stock pot to make the pizza sauce. Cook onions and garlic for 5-10 minutes in olive oil. Bring tomato puree and seasonings (basil through pepper flakes) to a boil, and reduce heat. Cover and cook for 30 minutes. Blend in batches or use an immersion blender to create a smoother sauce.

4. Bring to a boil. Reduce heat to low and simmer covered until desired consistency is achieved (reduced by 1/4- 1/3). This can vary depending on whether you used fresh or frozen tomatoes. Stir frequently to prevent sticking. If you use a thick-bottomed stockpot, stir more often to avoid scorching.

5. To can, add the lemon juice/citric acid to each clean, hot jar. Fill jars with sauce, leaving 1/2 inch headspace. Attach lids and rings until the seal is achieved. Put in canner rack. Repeat with the remaining jars until you are satisfied.

6. In a boiling water canner, process both half-pints and pints for 35 min.

7. Transfer to a towel-lined surface. Allow it to sit for 24 hours without any interruptions. Then, check seals and labeling, and store them in a cool, dark area, can be kept for up to a year.

Kcal	Fat	Carbs	Sugars	Fibers	Proteins	Salt
85	0 g	11 g	10 g	2 g	6 g	0.1 g

Preserving Orange Hard Sauce

Preparation Time: 10 minutes

Ingredients:

- 1 1/2 cups powdered sugar (confectioner's sugar)
- 1/2 cup unsalted butter, room temp
- 2 tablespoons brandy, bourbon, rum, orange liqueur, or Cognac (your choice)
- 1 teaspoon of orange zest (peel), finely grated

Instructions:

1. Mix butter and powdered sugar with an electric mixer until light and fluffy.

2. Add the vodka of your choice, and then add the grated orange peel. Stir until well combined.

3. Cover with plastic wrap and place in the refrigerator until you are ready to serve. Before serving, bring to room temperature.

Nutritional Values Per Serving

Kcal	Fat	Carbs	Sugars	Fibers	Proteins	Salt
61	0 g	2 g	10 g	2 g	6 g	0.1 g

Preserving Marshmallow Fluff Homemade

Preparation Time: 35 minutes

Ingredients for 1 large bowl:

- 3 eggs whites, room temperature

- 2 cups light corn syrup
- 1/2 teaspoon salt
- 2 cups powdered sugar (confectioners sugar)
- 1 tablespoon of pure vanilla extract

Instructions:

1. Add egg whites, corn syrup, and salt to a large bowl with an electric mixer.
2. Mix the mixture on high speed with your electric mixer for about 5 minutes, or until it becomes thicker and has nearly doubled volume.
3. Mix until smooth. Reduce mixer speed to low. Add powdered sugar. Mix in vanilla extract and mix until combined.
4. Now you can use your homemade marshmallow cream/fluff in your favorite recipes. You can either use it immediately or let it cool in a container for 2 weeks.

Nutritional Values Per Serving

Kcal	Fat	Carbs	Sugars
100	8 g	5 g	1 g

Fibers	Proteins	Sodium	Cholesterol
2 g	4 g	210 mg	5 mg

Preserving Broccoli Pesto Pasta

Preparation Time: 20 minutes

Cooking Time: 15 minutes

Ingredients For 6 Servings:

- 1 lb cooked pasta of your choosing, reserved pasta water
- 4 cups broccoli florets
- 2 cups basil leaves, lightly packaged
- 2 cloves of garlic
- 1/4 cup pine nuts
- 1 cup extra virgin olive oil
- 1/2 teaspoon salt
- 1 cup Parmigiano-Reggiano, grated

Instructions:

1. Bring water to a boil in a large saucepan.

2. Bring the water to a boil and add the broccoli. Don't drain the water. Transfer the broccoli immediately to a colander. Place under cold running water to stop further cook.

3. Bring the water to a boil. Add your pasta to the pot and cook according to the instructions.

4. Blend the following ingredients in a blender or food processor: basil, garlic, pine nuts, and olive oil. Add salt to taste. Slowly add 1 cup of the reserved pasta water to make a smooth sauce. You can add more pasta water if the sauce becomes too thick.

5. Mix the sauce with the hot pasta until it is well coated. If desired, top with additional Parmesan cheese, pine nuts, and chili flakes. Enjoy!

6. Salting your water before adding the pasta and broccoli is crucial. You can adjust the salt to suit your taste.

7. Keep covered in plastic wrap and place in the refrigerator until you are ready to serve, it can last for up to 3 months.

Nutritional Values Per Serving

Kcal	Fat	Carbs	Sugars
98	8 g	4 g	1 g

Fibers	Proteins	Sodium	Cholesterol
2 g	3 g	210 mg	5 mg

Preserving Cocktail Sauce

Preparation Time: 10 minutes

Ingredients:

- 1/2 cup chili sauce, catsup (ketchup)
- 2 tablespoons horseradish-style hot cream
- 1/4 teaspoon granulated Sugar
- 1 teaspoon coarse salt
- 1/2 teaspoon freshly cracked black pepper
- 2 teaspoons freshly squeezed lemon juice
- 4 crops Tabasco or your favorite hot sauce
- 1/2 teaspoon Worcestershire Sauce
- 2 cloves of garlic, minced

Instructions:

1. Mix all ingredients in a small bowl. Add more or less according to your taste.
2. Keep covered in plastic wrap and place in the refrigerator until you are ready to serve, it can last for up to 5 months.

Nutritional Values Per Serving

Kcal	Fat	Carbs	Sugars	Fibers	Proteins	Sodium
80	0 g	19 g	16 g	0.966 g	1 g	821 mg

Preserving Three Ingredient Tomato Sauce

Preparation Time: 5 minutes

Cooking Time: 30 minutes

Ingredients For 8 Servings:

- 4 lb ripe tomatoes, preferably Roma, with stem and core removed
- 1 cup olive oil
- 2 teaspoons salt
- *Optional: 3-5 fresh basil leaves*

Instructions:

1. Combine all ingredients in a large saucepan. Heat on medium/low heat. To help the tomatoes break down, smash the tomatoes with a spoon once it starts to bubble.
2. To avoid overcooking, cook the tomatoes for 30 mins. Stir frequently. The sauce should be thick. Continue cooking for a few minutes if the sauce is too thin.
3. If fresh basil is what you want to add, put 3-5 leaves in the pot.
4. Keep it in an airtight container for up to one week.

Nutritional Values Per Serving

Kcal	Fat	Carbs	Sugars
280	27 g	9 g	6 g

Fibers	Proteins	Sodium	Cholesterol
3 g	2 g	593 mg	0 mg

Preserving Spicy Chile Pepper Sauce

Preparation Time: 20 minutes

Cooking Time: 10 minutes

Ingredients For 1 Serving:

- 1 red bell pepper
- 3 Guajillo chile peppers, dried
- 5 Arbol chile peppers
- 6 cloves of garlic (skins removed)
- 1 teaspoon Caraway seeds
- 1 teaspoon of coriander seed
- 1 teaspoon cumin seeds
- 1 teaspoon coarse salt
- 1 teaspoon paprika, smoked

Instructions:

1. The whole bell pepper can be placed either on a flame or under the broiler at your stove to char the skin. Cover the entire bell pepper with plastic wrap and steam it for about 10 minutes. The charred skin of the pepper should be removed. Place the bell pepper pieces in a food processor.

2. Take the stems out of the dried chile peppers. You can either shake the seeds out or use a spoon to scrape them. Let the chile peppers sit in a bowl of water for 45 minutes. After the chile peppers have been dehydrated, please place them in a bowl with two tablespoons of water.

3. Use a mortar and pestle or a spice grinder to grind the garlic, toasted caraway, coriander, cumin, salt, and smoked paprika into a paste. Blend the paste with the bell pepper chunks and dried chile peppers in a food processor until smooth.

4. The sauce can be stored in the refrigerator for up to 6 months.

Nutritional Values Per Serving

Kcal	Fat	Carbs	Sugars
88	8 g	4 g	1 g

Fibers	Proteins	Sodium	Cholesterol
2 g	3 g	210 mg	5 mg

Home Preserved Cajun Chow Relish

Preparation Time: 20 minutes

Cooking Time: 2 hours

Ingredients:

- 2 finely chopped sweet onions
- 1 stalk celery, finely chopped
- 5 hot red chile peppers (preferably Cayenne Chili Peppers)
- 2 cups cider vinegar
- 1 tablespoon salt
- 1 teaspoon granulated Sugar

Instructions:

1. Mix and process the onion, celery, and chile peppers in a food processor.

2. Place the vegetable mixture in a saucepan on medium heat. Heat it just until it boils. Turn heat to low, and simmer for about 2 hours, stirring occasionally. Let cool on the stove.

3. Serve chilled or at room temp.

4. Refrigerate until you are ready to use it.

Nutritional Values Per Serving

Kcal	Fat	Carbs	Sugars
98	8 g	4 g	1 g

Fibers	Proteins	Sodium	Cholesterol
2 g	3 g	210 mg	5 mg

JELLIES

Preserving Honey Sweetened Jalapeno Gel

Preparation Time: 50 minutes

Cooking Time: 20 minutes

Ingredients For 8 Half-Pint Jars:

- 3 1/2 cups chopped jalapeno peppers, approximately 2 pounds
- 1 1/2 cups chopped Anaheim or Ancho peppers, approximately 1 to 1 1/4 lbs
- 1 1/4 cups cider vinegar
- 3 tablespoons Ball Low, No Sugar
- 2 1/2 cups honey

Instructions:

1. Keep warm up to 8 half-pints (8 ounces) jars. Set aside the lids and rings. Wash them in soapy water—boil water to make a canner.
2. In a large stockpot, combine the vinegar and peppers. Then slowly stir in the pectin.

3. Mix the mixture constantly and bring it to a boil on high heat. Do not stir.

4. Bring to a boil, add honey, and simmer for 3 minutes. Stir constantly. If necessary, remove from heat and skim any foam.

5. Hot jelly should be ladled into hot jars. Wipe the rim and place the lid on the pot. Attach the ring to the jar by tightening the screws until snug. Add a rack to the canner.

6. Lower the canning rack and let jars cool in the canner for 10 minutes (after boiling water has come to a boil with jars submerged). Turn off the burner and remove the lid. Let the jars cool in the canner for five minutes.

7. To cool for 24 hours, place jars on a towel-covered surface. Before storing, remove rings and check seals.

8. Label the jars and keep them in a dry, cool place for one year.

Nutritional Values Per Serving

Kcal	Fat	Carbs	Sugars
28	0.1 g	7.2 g	6.7 g

Fibers	Proteins	Sodium	Cholesterol
0.3 g	0.2 g	136 mg	0 mg

Preserving Blackberry Jelly

Preparation Time: 20 minutes

Cooking Time: 10 minutes

Ingredients For 6-Ounce Jars:

- 10 cups fresh blackberries
- 1 (1 3/4-ounce) package dry pectin
- 5 cups granulated sugar

Equipment required:

- Large boiling water canning pan with rack
- Non-reactive 6-8-quart saucepan
- Canning jars
- Rings for lilies
- Jar Grabber
- Jar Funnel

- Large spoon and ladle
- Jelly Bag, cheesecloth-lined Sieve

Instructions:

1. Preparing the equipment For a canner load with pint jars, fill the canner to half-full with warm water. You will need to adjust the water level to fill other sizes or numbers of jars. Use hot soapy water to wash jars, rings, and lids. Rinse with warm water.

2. Clean the rings, lids, and jars. Avoid putting pots that are room temperature into boiling water. They may crack. Place the jars into a large saucepan. Cover the jars with 1-inch water and let it simmer for 10 minutes. The hot water will heat the rings, lids, and jars until they are ready for use.

3. Preparing the blackberries. Wash, stem, and drain the blackberries. Remove any stems and cores. To lightly crush the blackberries, use a potato masher or food mill. Crush only one cup at a given time for best results. To make 3 1/2 cups of blackberry juice, use a jelly bag or cheesecloth-lined sieve.

4. Add sugar and dry pectin. Mix well by stirring. *NOTE: Jelly setting will not be successful if you reduce sugar or use sugar substitutes.* You must use the Pectin with Less Sugar or Zero Sugar to reduce sugar. Continue stirring, and bring to a full rolling boil. Boil for 1 minute, stirring continuously. A rolling boil can't be stirred down. It will reduce foaming if you bring the mixture back to a spot slowly (on medium heat instead of high). Take it off the heat and immediately skim any foam/bubbles.

5. One at a time, pour the jelly into sterilized containers. If you use self-sealing lids, fill to the top. Use a damp cloth to wipe the rim of the jars or glasses. Place a hot lid on top of the container and secure the ring.

6. Process the jelly by placing jars on an elevated rack. The hot water will be used to lower the frame into the canner. If necessary, add more boiling water to make sure the water level is not below the tops of the jars. The water should be poured around the pots, not

directly on them. Cover the canner with a lid. Cover the canner with a lid and boil for 10 minutes.

7. Take the jars out with a jar lifter after 10 minutes. Place them on a cooling rack or towel to cool completely. Keep at least 1 inch between the jars while cooling. The pots should not be placed on a cold surface or under a draft. Allow the jars to cool for 12-24 hours. Keep the lids loose and not press down on the metal lid's center until the pot has cooled completely.

8. Check seals after jars have cooled. Press the middle of the lid with your finger. If a cover does not spring back, refrigeration is required. Use any unsealed containers first before putting them in the fridge.

9. Label the jars and keep them in a dry, cool place for one year. Keep open jars in the refrigerator for up to three weeks.

Nutritional Values Per Serving

Kcal	Fat	Carbs	Sugars
23	0.1 g	7 g	6.8 g

Fibers	Proteins	Sodium	Cholesterol
0.3 g	0.2 g	131 mg	0 mg

Preserving Lavender Jelly

Preparation Time: 20 minutes

Cooking Time: 30 minutes

Ingredients For 1/2 Pints:

- 3 1/2 cups of water
- 1/2 cup lavender flowers, dried
- 1 lemon juice (approximately 1/4 cup)
- 1 (3/4-ounce) Box Pectin, powdered; 1 (3/4-ounces) Pouch (3-ounces), liquid pectin
- 4 cups sugar (granulated)

Equipment required:

- Large boiling water canning pan with rack
- Non-reactive 6-8-quart saucepan
- Canning jars

- Lids with rings- Metal bands attach the covers to the containers. You can reuse the rounds many times but only 1 cap
- Jar Grabber
- Jar Funnel
- Large spoon and ladle
- Jelly Bag, cheesecloth-lined Sieve

Instructions:

1. Preparing the equipment For a canner load with pint jars, fill the canner to half-full with warm water. You will need to adjust the water level to fill other sizes or numbers of jars. Use hot soapy water to wash jars, rings, and lids. Rinse with warm water.

2. Clean the rings, lids, and jars. Place the jars into a large saucepan. Cover the jars with 1-inch water and let it boil for 10 minutes. The hot water will heat the rings, lids, and jars until they are ready for use.

3. Prepare the lavender jelly by heating water in a large saucepan. Stir in the dried lavender flowers and allow them to steep for 20 minutes. Strain the mixture into a large pot or kettle and discard the lavender flowers. Mix in the lemon juice and pectin. Continue stirring until the pectin dissolves. Bring the mixture to boil over high heat. Add sugar. Let the jelly solution return to a boil over high heat. Stir occasionally.

Boil Times:

- 2 minutes: soft gel
- 4 minutes: medium gel

1. To test for "jell thickness," I place a tablespoon of metal in ice water. Then, I take half a spoonful of the mixture and allow it to cool to room temperature. The jelly is ready

when it thickens to the consistency that I prefer. If it doesn't, I add a bit more pectin (1 teaspoon to 1/2 cup from another package) to the mixture and bring it back to a boil for one minute.

2. Process the jelly by placing jars on an elevated rack. The hot water will be used to lower the shelf into the canner. If necessary, add more boiling water to make sure the water level is not below the tops of the jars. The water should be poured around the pots, not directly on them. Cover the canner with a lid. Put the lid on the canner and boil for 10 minutes. Allow jars to cool for 10 minutes. Allow at least 1 inch between the jars to cool. The pots should not be placed on a cold surface or under a draft. Allow the jars to cool for 12-24 hours. Keep the lids loose and not press down on the metal lid's center until the pot has cooled completely.

3. Check seals after jars have cooled. Press the middle of the lid with your finger. If the top does not spring back, refrigeration is required. Use any unsealed containers first before putting them in the fridge.

4. Label the jars and keep them in a dry, cool place for one year. Keep open jars in the refrigerator for up to three weeks.

Nutritional Values Per Serving

Kcal	Fat	Carbs	Sugars
28	0 g	7.2 g	6.7 g

Fibers	Proteins	Sodium	Cholesterol
0.3 g	0.2 g	136 mg	0 mg

Preserving Perada Pear Jelly

Preparation Time: 5 minutes

Cooking Time: 2 hours

Ingredients For Serving 16 Ounces of Jelly:

- 6 to 7 medium-sized pears, firm (leave the skin on)
- 2 1/2 cups superfine sugar or caster sugar
- 7 ounces of water
- 1/2 lemon juice
- *4 tablespoons liquid pectin (optional)*

Instructions:

1. Rinse the pear. Any bruises or other problems (bruises, etc.) should be removed. The stalks can be removed, but the skin should remain.
2. Boil the pears whole in boiling water until they are soft. Let cool on a plate.

3. While the skin is still warm, peel it off. Use a food mill, a metal spoon, or a wire mesh strainer to mash the pear pulp. Three cups should be enough to make pear puree.

4. You should use about 3/4 of the puree sugar. In 7 ounces of water, dissolve the sugar. Let the syrup boil for about ten minutes until it reaches 218°F. Next, add the lemon juice, pear purée, and liquid pectin, if necessary. Cook, stirring, for about 5 minutes. Once it has reached a rapid boil, reduce heat to medium and simmer for another few minutes. Stirring occasionally until the mixture thickens, cook for about an hour, making sure it doesn't stick to the bottom. The mix will be ready when it pulls away from the sides of the pan.

5. Fill molds, bowls, or hot sterile jam containers. Allow cooling completely before placing in the refrigerator until set.

6. *NOTE: To make the parade hold its shape during slicing, you can add liquid pectin to the pears or cook an apple.* Pears are low in pectin, allowing the caravan to set completely before being cut. Allow cooling in molds. After the mixture has cooled completely, remove from molds and cut.

7. Serve immediately, or Keep it in the refrigerator for up to five months.

Nutritional Values Per Serving

Kcal	Fat	Carbs	Sugars	Fibers	Proteins	Sodium
40	0 g	10 g	9.2 g	0.7 g	0.1 g	0.6 mg

JAMS

Preserving Fig Jam

Preparation Time: 15 minutes

Cooking Time: 35 minutes

Ingredients For 25 Servings:

- 1 kg figs
- 3/4 cup orange juice
- 1/4 cup lemon juice
- 1 kg sugar warmed
- *Optional: 2 tsp of sweet sherry*

Equipment:

- 1 saucepan
- 2 glass jars with lid

Instructions:

1. Wash the figs and cut off any stems. Then chop them roughly. Combine juice and sherry in a large saucepan.
2. Bring to a boil. Reduce heat and simmer until the figs are tender.
3. Stir in the warm sugar, and heat on low until it dissolves.
4. Boil covered for 25 minutes or until jam is set when you test it on a cold saucer.
5. Place in hot sterilized jars.
6. Label the jars and keep them in a dry, cool place for one year.

Nutritional Values Per Serving

Kcal	Fat	Carbs	Sugars	Fibers	Proteins	Salt
49	0 g	11 g	11 g	1 g	0.4 g	0.02 g

Preserving Rose Petal Jam

Preparation Time: 10 minutes

Cooking Time: 25 minutes

Ingredients For 1 Serving:

- 1/2 pound pink, red or edible rose petals
- 2 cups granulated sugar, split
- 4 1/2 cups of water
- 1 cup of freshly squeezed lemons

Instructions:

1. Remove bitter white bases and cut rose petals. Rinse petals well and drain.
2. Sprinkle enough sugar on each rose petal to cover it. Allow setting for at least one night.
3. Place remaining sugar, water, lemon juice, and salt in a saucepan. Stir to dissolve sugar. Let simmer for 20 minutes before stirring in the rose petals. Turn heat up to

medium-high. Bring mixture to a boil. Continue boiling for 5 minutes or until the mixture thickens. Turn off the heat.

4. Once the jam has been boiled, pour it into sterilized jars. Fill them to 1/4 inch below the top. Clean any spot from the top. Place the lid on the lid and secure the ring. Label, cover, and keep in an excellent location for one year

Nutritional Values Per Serving

Kcal	Fat	Carbs	Sugars
35.49	3.94 g	11.63 g	6.7 g

Fibers	Proteins	Sodium	Cholesterol
0.4 g	4.08 g	23.26 mg	0 mg

Preserving Blackberry Jam

Preparation Time: 20 minutes

Cooking Time: 10 minutes

Ingredients For 9 Serving:

- 5 cups of prepared blackberries
- 7 cups granulated sugar
- 1 (1 3/4-ounce) package/box fruit pectin
- *1/2 teaspoon butter (optional)*

Equipment required:

- Large boiling water canning pan with rack
- Non-reactive 6-8-quart saucepan

- Canning jars
- Lids with rings- Metal bands attach the covers to the containers. You can reuse the rounds many times but only the top
- Jar grabber
- Jar funnel
- Large spoon and ladle

Instructions:

1. Jam is only made in small batches (roughly 6 cups).
2. Preparing the equipment For a canner load with pint jars, fill the canner to half-full with warm water. You will need to adjust the water level to fill other sizes or numbers of jars. Use hot soapy water to wash jars, rings, and lids. Rinse with warm water.
3. Clean the rings, lids, and jars. Avoid putting pots that are room temperature into boiling water. They may crack. Place the jars into a large saucepan. Cover the jars with 1-inch water and let it simmer for 10 minutes. The hot water will heat the rings, lids, and jars until they are ready for use.
4. Preparing the blackberries.
5. To lightly crush the blackberries, use a potato masher or food mill. You will get the best results if you destroy only one cup at a given time.
6. Make the jam by measuring the sugar in a separate bowl and putting it in a separate bowl. *NOTE: Using sugar substitutes or reducing sugar will cause the knot not to be set up correctly.* You must use the pectin with Less Sugar or Zero Sugar to reduce sugar.
7. In a large 6- to 8-quart saucepan, measure the exact amount of blackberries (juice). In the blackberry mixture, stir in 1 box/package of fruit pectin. If desired, add 1/2 teaspoon butter to reduce foaming.

8. Bring mixture to a rolling boil over high heat. Stir constantly. A full rolling boil does not stop bubbling after being stirred. Add the sugar quickly and stir. Let boil for 1 minute, stirring frequently.

9. It will reduce foaming if you bring the mixture back to a boil slowly (on medium heat instead of high).

10. Take off heat immediately and skim any foam/bubbles.

11. Put jam in the jars. Place one pot at a. time in the hot prepared spot in the sterilized jars. Fill the jars to 1/8 inch below the top. Use a damp cloth to wipe the rim of the pot or glass. Place a hot lid on top of the container and secure the ring.

12. Process the jam by placing the jars on an elevated rack. The hot water will be used to lower the frame into the canner. If necessary, add more boiling water to make sure the water level is not below the tops of the jars. The water should be poured around the pots, not directly on them. Cover the canner with a lid. Put the lid on the canner and boil for 10 minutes. You can adjust the processing time based on the altitude chart.

13. Allow jars to cool for 10 minutes. Allow at least 1 inch between the jars to cool. The pots should not be placed on a cold surface or under a draft. Allow the jars to cool for 12-24 hours. Keep the lids loose and not press down on the metal lid's center until the pot has cooled completely.

14. Check seals after jars have cooled. Press the middle of the lid with your finger. If a cover does not spring back, refrigeration is required. Use any unsealed containers first before putting them in the fridge.

15. Label the jars and keep them in a dry, cool place for one year. Keep open jars in the refrigerator for up to three weeks.

Nutritional Values Per Serving

Kcal	Fat	Carbs	Sugars	Fibers	Proteins	Sodium
50	1 g	13 g	12 g	0.4 g	0 g	0 mg

MARMALADES

Preserving Sweet and Spicy Onion Marmalade

Preparation Time: 30 minutes

Cooking Time: 10 minutes

Ingredients For 6 Half-Pints:

- 2 lb onions, sweet or regular
- 1 cup apple juice
- 1/2 cup cider vinegar
- 2 teaspoons of minced fresh garlic
- 1 teaspoon salt
- 1/2 teaspoon black pepper
- 1/4 teaspoon ground mustard
- 1 teaspoon crushed red pepper flakes
- 3 tablespoons Low Sugar or No Sugar Needed Pectin - Flex batch equals 1 Box
- 1 cup of honey
- 1/2 cup brown sugar
- *1 teaspoon of butter or oil i(optional)*

Instructions:

1. Make a water bath canner and 6 half-pint jars with lids. Keep warm until you need them.

2. Ends of onions should be removed. Peel the onions then cut in half lengthwise. If onions are large, you can also engrave them in thirds. Cut in 1/4 inch slices lengthwise from the halves. Pieces should be placed in an 8-quart measuring cup. You should have 6 cups.

3. In a 8-quart stockpot, combine prepared onions, apple juice vinegar, garlic, salt and pepper, red pepper flakes, mustard, and vinegar. Add pectin gradually and, if necessary, butter. Stir constantly as you bring the mixture to a boil.

4. Bring to boil honey and sugar. Let boil for one minute, stirring continuously. If necessary, remove from heat and skim foam.

5. Hot marmalade in prepared half-pint jars, one at a. Place in a canner.

6. Cover the canner with a lid and bring to a gentle boil—Cook for 10 minutes. Keep the spot going. Turn off the heat and allow jars to cool in the canner for 5 minutes. Then, transfer pots to a towel-lined surface to cool down for 24 hours. Before labeling, check the seal of the lids and store them in a dark, cool place with no rings. It will keep in the refrigerator for about 2 to 3 months.

Nutritional Values Per Serving

Kcal	Fat	Carbs	Sugars	Fibers	Proteins	Sodium
26	0 g	6.6 g	5.7 g	0.4 g	0.2 g	32 mg

Preserving Pickling and Canning Asparagus

Preparation Time: 40 minutes

Cooking Time: 10 minutes

Ingredients For 7 Pints:

- Asparagus weighing between 10 and 12 pounds
- 7 large cloves of garlic, cut in half
- 5 cups of water
- 5 cups vinegar
- 5 tablespoons pickling/canning salt
- 4 tablespoons sugar

Optional additions per jar:

- ½ teaspoon whole peppercorns
- ¼ teaspoon red pepper flake

Instructions:

1. Use hot water and soap to clean 7-ounce jars or 12-ounce jars. Warm canner water is an excellent choice to keep the clean jars warm.

2. Preparing asparagus: Place one spear in a container and slice it to 1/2 inch below the top. Then, use this as a guide for cutting the rest of the asparagus. Before you proceed, make sure that all asparagus is cut.

3. Bring 1/2 to 3/4 of the water into a water-bath container and boil it.

4. In a large non-reactive saucepan, add vinegar, sugar, and canning salt. Mix well and bring to boil.

5. Place a garlic clove, red pepper flakes, and *optional peppercorns in each jar*. Then fill the jars with spears. They will shrink when heated, so pack them tightly.

6. Fill each jar with the hot vinegar mixture at an a.m., leaving 1/2 inch headspace. Use a non-metal spatula to remove air bubbles, then replace the brine. Finally, wipe the rim with damp towels.

7. Attach the lid to the ring and tighten until you feel the fingertip.

8. Each jar should be lowered as you place it in the canner. Fill each jar until you are done.

9. Bring the canner over high heat to a rolling boil. Set the timer for 10 seconds and adjust the heat to keep the canner at a gentle boil.

10. Turn off the burner when the timer goes off. Remove the lid and allow the jars to rest for five minutes. Each jar can be lifted using the jar lifter. Allow sleeping for 24 hours. Make sure to check the lids and seals. If you don't have the seals on the jars, keep them in the refrigerator. The rest of the pots can be stored in a relaxed and dark place. Jars should be used within one year.

Nutritional Values Per Serving

Kcal	Fat	Satured	Carbs
49	0.2 g	0.1 g	8.7 g

Sugars	Fibers	Proteins	Sodium
4.9 g	3.4 g	3.6 g	318 mg

Preserving Onion Marmalade

Preparation Time: 20 minutes

Cooking Time: 1 hour

Ingredients For 12 Servings:

- 3 large, red or white onions, peeled and cut in half. Then thinly sliced
- 1/2 cup olive oil
- 1 teaspoon sea salt or coarse salt

- 1/2 teaspoon freshly ground black pepper
- 2 bay leaves
- 2 rosemary sprigs
- 2 tablespoons of soft brown sugar. You can add more or decrease it to suit your tastes
- 1/3 cup dry red wine
- 1/3 cup red wine vinegar
- 1/8 cup Balsamic Vinegar (good quality)

Instructions:

1. The stem and root ends should be removed. Next, cut the onions half lengthwise and peel off the dried skin. Slice the onions into 1/4 inch slices. All onion slices must be roughly equal in size to ensure even cooking. Your pot will now be full of sliced onion slices. However, the onions will shrink and wilt during cooking.

2. Heat the olive oil in a large, heavy skillet on medium heat. Toss in the chopped onions and drizzle olive oil over them. Cook covered on medium heat until onions turn golden brown. Add the salt and pepper, bay leaves, rosemary, and stir. Stirring occasionally, cook for 20-30 minutes, or until the herbs are wilted.

3. Mix in the wine, vinegar, and balsamic vinegar. Bring to a boil and stir constantly. Then reduce the heat to low and simmer for 20-30 minutes, or until the liquid has dissolved and the onions become soft and sticky. TIP: Stir continuously throughout this process to ensure that the onions don't stick to the bottom of your pan or become burned.

4. Take out the bay and rosemary leaves.

5. You can now serve the Onion Marmalade. It will taste even better if it has mellowed for at least two weeks. The onion marmalade can be stored for 6 months if it is immediately put into sterilized glass preservation jars, sealed, and left to cool in the fridge for 3 days.

Kcal	Fat	Saturated	Carbs
180	9 g	1 g	23 g

Sugars	Fibers	Proteins	Sodium
19 g	1 g	1 g	184 mg

Orange Marmalade

Preparation Time: 1 hour

Cooking Time: 30 minutes

Ingredients For 1 Serving:

- 300 ml orange juice (approx 5 Kinnow Oranges)
- 200 gr orange pulp
- 60 gr orange rind, julienned

- 250 gr granulated white sugar
- 1 tablespoon lime juice

Ingredients To Clean Oranges:

- 1 teaspoon baking soda
- water

Instructions:

1. Add a teaspoon of baking soda to water. Wash the oranges with the skin in baking soda water. Pat dry with a clean kitchen towel.
2. Cut the oranges in half. Using a sharp fruit knife remove seeds from oranges.
3. Using a citrus juicer squeeze out the juice from the oranges. Scoop out the pulp in a separate bowl. Discard white pith, seeds, or transparent skin covering the pulp. Combine juice and pulp. Total they should be 500 gram (300 ml Juice + 200 gram Pulp).
4. Using a spoon remove the white pith inside the rind. It tastes bitter and spoils the marmalade. Now, julienne the orange rind or cut it into thin strips. It should be 60 gram. You can use the rind of two oranges.
5. Add sugar, line juice, and mix. Cover and keep aside. After 15 minutes, sugar will be completely dissolved with the fruit. Do not rush this process.
6. Start cooking the marmalade in a heavy-duty ceramic, enamel, steel, or glass saucepan.
7. Stage 1, the marmalade will be watery, and white foam on top. Keep cooking on low heat, while stirring at regular intervals.
8. Slowly, the white foam will start reducing, the texture of the marmalade would thicken a bit. Use a potato masher or a ladle to gently mash the pulp and orange rind.
9. After 20 minutes on low heat, the white foam on top will disappear, pulp mashed nicely, and the marmalade will start sticking to the spoon. Turn off the heat.

10. Take a big spoonful of marmalade and spread it on a plate. It should be sticky and not watery with a sheen to it. That is the signal that marmalade is ready!

11. Allow the marmalade to cool down completely at room temperature. Store the cooled marmalade in a clean, sterilised glass jar with a tight-fitting lid freeze and use within 6 months to one year.

Nutritional Values Per Serving

Kcal	Fat	Saturated	Carbs	Sugars
3	1 g	1 g	1 g	1 g

Fibers	Proteins	Sodium	Potassium
1 g	1 g	2 mg	2 mg

APPENDIX: TABLE OF MEASUREMENTS AND CONVERSIONS

BASIC KITCHEN CONVERSIONS & EQUIVALENTS

DRY MEASUREMENTS CONVERSION CHART

3 TEASPOONS = 1 TABLESPOON = 1/16 CUP
6 TEASPOONS = 2 TABLESPOONS = 1/8 CUP
12 TEASPOONS = 4 TABLESPOONS = ¼ CUP
24 TEASPOONS = 8 TABLESPOONS = ½ CUP
36 TEASPOONS = 12 TABLESPOONS = ¾ CUP
48 TEASPOONS = 16 TABLESPOONS = 1 CUP

LIQUID MEASUREMENTS CONVERSION CHART

8 FLUID OUNCES = 1 CUP = ½ PINT
    = ¼ QUART
16 FLUID OUNCES = 2 CUPS = 1 PINT
    = ½ QUART
32 FLUID OUNCES = 4 CUPS = 2 PINTS
    = 1 QUART = ¼ GALLON
128 FLUID OUNCES = 16 CUPS = 8 PINTS
    = 4 QUARTS = 1 GALLON

BUTTER

1 CUP BUTTER = 2 STICKS = 8 OUNCES
    = 230 GRAMS = 8 TABLESPOONS

METRIC TO US COOKING CONVERSIONS

OVEN TEMPERATURES

120 C = 250 F
160 C = 320 F
180 C = 350 F
205 C = 400 F
220 C = 425 F

BAKING IN GRAMS

1 CUP FLOUR = 140 GRAMS
1 CUP SUGAR = 150 GRAMS
1 CUP POWDERED SUGAR = 160 GRAMS
1 CUP HEAVY CREAM = 235 GRAMS

VOLUME

1 MILLILITER = 1/5 TEASPOON
5 ML = 1 TEASPOON
15 ML = 1 TABLESPOON
240 ML = 1 CUP OR 8 FLUID OUNCES
1 LITER = 34 FL. OUNCES

WEIGHT

1 GRAM = .035 OUNCES
100 GRAMS = 3.5 OUNCES
500 GRAMS = 1.1 POUNDS
1 KILOGRAM = 35 OUNCES

US TO METRIC COOKING CONVERSIONS

1/5 TSP = 1 ML
1 TSP = 5 ML
1 TBSP = 15 ML
1 FL OUNCE = 30 ML
1 CUP = 237 ML
1 PINT (2 CUPS) = 473 ML
1 QUART (4 CUPS) = .95 LITER
1 GALLON (16 CUPS) = 3.8 LITERS
1 OZ = 28 GRAMS
1 POUND = 454 GRAMS

WHAT DOES 1 CUP EQUAL ?

1 CUP = 8 FLUID OUNCES
1 CUP = 16 TABLESPOONS
1 CUP = 48 TEASPOONS
1 CUP = ½ PINT
1 CUP = ¼ QUART
1 CUP = 1/16 GALLON
1 CUP = 240 ML

BAKING PAN CONVERSIONS

9-INCH ROUND CAKE PAN = 12 CUPS
10-INCH TUBE PAN = 16 CUPS
10-INCH BUNDT PAN = 12 CUPS
9-INCH SPRINGFORM PAN = 10 CUPS
9 X 5 INCH LOAF PAN = 8 CUPS
9-INCH SQUARE PAN = 8 CUPS

BAKING PAN CONVERSIONS

1 CUP ALL-PURPOSE FLOUR = 4.5 OZ
1 CUP ROLLED OATS = 3 OZ
1 LARGE EGG = 1.7 OZ
1 CUP BUTTER = 8 OZ
1 CUP MILK = 8 OZ
1 CUP HEAVY CREAM = 8.4 OZ
1 CUP GRANULATED SUGAR = 7.1 OZ
1 CUP PACKED BROWN SUGAR = 7.75 OZ
1 CUP VEGETABLE OIL = 7.7 OZ
1 CUP UNSIFTED POWDERED SUGAR = 4.4 OZ

REFERENCES

Peterson, S, Home Canning Recipes. List of canning tutorials. Retrieved from:

https://www.simplycanning.com/home-canning-recipes/

Jen, (2021). Home Food Canning: The Benefits Retrieved from:

https://www.inspiringsavings.com/the-benefits-of-home-canning-your-own-food/

Wilfred, N, food preservation. Retrieved from: https://www.britannica.com/topic/food-preservation